Mighty Mites

Dedication   Without the support of so many fantastic and influential people in my life, guiding me through experiences which educate, sculpt, and give joy, something like this book adventure would not have been possible. It has been a defining part of my life, allowing me to hopefully assist the many on changing a youth soccer culture for the better, and I want to thank those who without their support, this wouldn't have happened.

To all of my family and friends from back home in England: people like my mum, dad, and sister, and friends like Dan, Wayne, and John. People who do things like plan a whole wedding for a guy who is only there once every other year. These are the people that allow me to leave my home, as I know I will always have a place where I belong whenever I need.

To my Japanese brother, Sugar, for somehow getting me to Montevallo University in Alabama, guiding my work ethic as a coach, and then introducing me to Coerver Coaching and Dave Dresbach. Dave will always be influential in allowing me to find my brand as a coach and educating me on the defining Coerver Methodology.

To my wife, Kim, and children Courtney, Garret, Kylie, and Gianna. As every married man knows, we are nothing without our better half supporting us and allowing us to wear the pants every now and then. Thank you to all of you for giving my life meaning and supporting me emotionally every day. I am forever thankful you are in my life. Your support and smiles make the bad days great and the great days perfect.

Thank you to all of the people along the way who have been there on and off the field. You are all in my heart and mind.

Finally, I would like to dedicate this book to my newborn son, Devon. I hope you live a full life and your soccer coaches in the future have read this book and give you a great platform to be the next England's no. 9. I love you with all my heart and I cannot wait to watch you grow into an outstanding man.

Chris Castell

MIGHTY MITES
Youth Soccer Session Plans
and Methodology for U4-U8

Meyer & Meyer Sport

British Library Cataloguing in Publication Data

A catalogue record for this book is available from the British Library

Mighty Mites

Maidenhead: Meyer & Meyer Sport (UK) Ltd.,
ISBN: 978-1-78255-016-7

Aachen, Auckland, Beirut, Budapest, Cairo, Cape Town, Dubai,
Hägendorf, Indianapolis, Singapore, Sydney, Tehran, Wien

Member of the World Sport Publishers' Association (WSPA)

Printed by: B.O.S.S Druck und Medien GmbH, Germany

ISBN: 978-1-78255-016-7

E-Mail: info@m-m-sports.com

www.m-m-sports.com

CONTENTS

CHAPTER ONE

INTRODUCTION

INTRODUCTION

Welcome one and all to the easiest and most efficient guide to youth soccer. If you are looking for the complete guide to developing your players at the highest rate, but you are concerned that this may be a difficult task, then you are in the right place. This easy, concise guide is the CliffsNotes guide to making creative and fun sessions which take your soccer players from amateur to professional in seconds. (Disclaimer: this book does not guarantee players will become professional, especially in seconds.) The main hope for this book is that you have a great time with your players as you teach the beautiful game of soccer, rather than the misconception that one can only be done in lieu of the other.

For most of us, the thought of coaching a young team is as daunting as a parent going through childbirth as the "what am I doing here" and "what am I supposed to do" questions are ringing in your ears. You are to take on the challenge of being a youth soccer coach, but do not fear and fret no more. Coaches, it's time to put on your combats and strap on that helmet. Let's go to work!

If you are reading this book, you are either: a club official, coach, or board member, assigned to lead your coaches in elite level youth coaching; or a coach, parent, or other, with some experience in soccer and set to be the head coach of a team; or a parent thrown in at the deep end with zero knowledge of soccer and coaching.

Whatever the reason, I am here to help.

Coaching, or asking young people to do anything, is pretty tough, so you are doing the right thing by researching what the best approach may be. This book will give you strategies and techniques to make the whole process as much fun for you as it will be for the players, so relax. As you read through the book, there are many new and revolutionary techniques used to give your sessions the best look and feel and to instill pride in what you are doing for these kids and the organization. To do this, with young, screaming, quiet, energetic, overenthusiastic, shy, bouncy kids is no mean feat, so it's time to take control!

When I research training sessions for the younger ages, I always have two major complaints. First of all, the coaches seem to forget that these are 4- to 6-year-old children, not infants who can barely walk. They have the potential to do so much and surprise everyone. We can teach them to hold a crayon properly, color within the lines, and even write their own name. Therefore, shouldn't we hold the same high expectations when teaching them how to properly kick a ball in a certain direction? And secondly, the same coaches do not seem to understand how difficult it is as coaches to maintain the attention, organize, and direct a group of young children into the drills. You may have one child punching another while Timmy is in the corner picking daisies, and George is running off the field to see mommy for a drink. Kids are not always easy to handle at that age, but there is, more often than not, nothing in the session plan to handle these challenges. Everything we do with the youth, we must take into account the possible personalities which we would encounter. So, how can we devise a session to be the catalyst for player development AND take into consideration their limited attention spans?

The answer is to give the children what they already love and add a ball. It's that simple. From there, you can teach anything you want!

CHAPTER TWO

COACHING APPROACH FOR USA AND EUROPE

COACHING APPROACH FOR USA AND EUROPE

A good analogy for learning soccer can come from looking at the school systems. Relate skill to subjects such as reading and math. Without these skills, we cannot excel in subjects such as history or science. We may be able to recite dates, but to become a History major, we must be able to apply our knowledge to paper. This is the same relation to skill and technique as in soccer. Without skill, all techniques (like passing and shooting) are difficult because our body and mind are not ready to compute all the actions we want to apply. If we teach skill first, however, technique becomes a by-product of this development. You may not be great at remembering dates in history, but you can at least describe what you are thinking effectively through your knowledge of the English language. Realistically, all general education classes can be compared to the techniques of the game. Geography, History, and Science are equivalent to passing, receiving, shooting, and so on. All of which are important, but we cannot get an A without a solid understanding and mastery of English or Math. We do not have to completely ignore the techniques as we learn the fundamental skills. Just like in school, children write about animals and personal and historical events. The majority of what they read and write about in school is about different subjects, but the teacher focuses on the application of English. We do the same in skill development. In my sessions, I have goals for players to shoot toward, passing and receiving to initiate the game and throughout, but my focus remains on the skill application.

Currently, the soccer community is completely backwards in most countries. At the younger ages, we give kids a ball and put a goal at each end and show them the game. Then they become a little more competent, so we teach them how to spread out and pass. After this, we get to the U8 level and realize the kids are lacking in individual ability, so we teach them how to dribble and perform skills and maneuvers with the ball. Now the player becomes a good individual player, we start to teach them tactics again at the U11 age or when they enter the elite level of soccer in the community. My questions to every coach or director of a program are these: Why do we first teach passing which leads to tactics? If a child is attempting to keep the ball, why do we tell them to pass it away to someone else? Wouldn't it be wiser to teach them how to keep the ball more skillfully and then build on the foundation they have?

CHAPTER
THREE

CHILD PSYCHOLOGY

CHILD PSYCHOLOGY

In order to be productive at any age group, you have to identify the target audience and figure out what they want. For instance, imagine giving your spouse a big cardboard box for Christmas, expecting them to play with it for hours pretending it's a space ship. The same works in reverse, as we cannot expect a child to be ecstatic with a diamond necklace, so what makes this target age group tick?

I have asked myself, "What seems to amuse nearly all children?" Clowns are the first things that come to mind, but why? Clowns have the ability to maintain the attention of a group of children for a decent period of time. They are always on the move, and you never know what to expect next. Why not incorporate this in our sessions? I'm not saying go out there in a clown outfit with a red nose and a flower that squirts water, but ensure you are the center of attention, stay on the move, and be random! If you see anyone misbehaving or losing focus, run to the other side of the area with the ball and ask them to follow. The majority of kids will always be intrigued and come with you. The others will follow as they don't want to be left out and alone. Certain techniques, such as asking players to put their hands on their knees, then head, feet, eyes, ending on their mouth (at a high tempo) will get their attention quickly (and also keep them quiet as they now have their hands over their mouth). This idea of you as the center of attention should be incorporated in each and every session and in as many games as possible.

With this in mind, from now on you have to become the best actor in the world, able to take on any role, adding humor along the way. In doing so, you are willing to make an absolute idiot of yourself in the process. (Think Jim Carey or Robin Williams, for instance.) To get you in the spirit, today you are the soldier, fighting in the soccer trenches with nothing but your whit and cunning to take on these young cadets and train them to become top soccer players. As your drill instructor, I will guide you in the art of war, giving you all the secret methods of how to have these uncompromising cadets eating out of the palm of your hand in no time. Before we get to the field and let you loose on these unsuspecting young soccer players, let us take a moment to understand our mission and why.

As far as youth entertainment, and adult entertainment for that matter, more money and time is spent on stories than anything else. We watch movies and TV shows as adults for pure entertainment. Most children are now mesmerized when you put Nickelodeon or a Disney movie on the big screen. So why do we talk to these young players about lining up behind a cone and expect them to care about it and, more to the point, understand the necessity as much as we do? My question to coaches is:

Can you take the same ideas and drills you want the children to learn and do, but make it fun at the same time?

CHAPTER FOUR

PHILOSOPHY OF SKILL DEVELOPMENT

PHILOSOPHY OF SKILL DEVELOPMENT

Coaching passing and receiving is easier than coaching skill. This is because most coaches do not have skill knowledge, nor know how to teach the skill by breaking the maneuver down further. Then add all the different play variables, such as reading the defender, timing of the skill or which foot to use and you have a daunting task ahead of you. My experience in skill development has given me a repertoire of over 150 different foot skills of which every one has a specific use in improving technical perfection and creating time and space to make better decisions. Understanding this, I want to give some of this knowledge to you, especially once you understand the bigger picture of global soccer.

The soccer world is crying out for technical players with pace. If you are technically sound, passing is easy. Think about the most skillful countries and players in the world. Most of these players possess the ball amazingly well! Is it because all they did was learn how to pass? Or is it because they are confident they can get out of any tight situation, often while keeping the ball?

As a defender, it would be foolish of me to try and pressure hard against a player who could potentially beat me 1-on-1. In this instance, my pressure is lower, giving the player on the ball more time and space and leading to easier possession. Patience is the key when defending a technically-skilled player. We need to change our coaching approach from teaching tactics/technique/tactics (passing, skill, passing) to the simpler technique/tactics. Do away with actual soccer goals in practice and replace them with targets (goals to represent an end product rather than scoring 'a goal') or gates to dribble through.. Take the emphasis away from winning and losing. Put the focus on individual brilliance at a younger age.

In all of the sessions here, the goals are used only once as you would see on a game day. We use them for shooting practice and as props in the session. I understand the need for scrimmaging at the end of a regular practice, as most players enjoy the release from the monotony of learning, and to some extent they need an opportunity to put the session ideals into a game-like format. However, if the whole practice is fun and full of games, what is the need to end the session with another game? The players should have a game day on the weekend, so do not feel obliged to give them more.

CHAPTER
FIVE

WHY AND HOW TO CREATE A YOUTH SESSION PLAN

WHY AND HOW TO CREATE A YOUTH SESSION PLAN

For any session, we as coaches and educators have a session plan where we start with the skills we want to teach, and then design a series of games or drills that incorporate them while trying to make them fun, too. For youth players, trying to take a skill and move along the unopposed (no pressure), semi-opposed (limited pressure), and opposed (full pressure) routes, we are asking too much of a young child who only wants to have a good time. Personally, I choose to work things the other way around. I take the fun aspect and put that as the base of the cake, not just the icing on top. My session topic is the name of the adventure on which I want to take the players, such as Funky Chicken Island. For example, the Hunt for the Funky Chicken is primarily a dribbling exercise. Save the Funky Chicken Egg is a passing, receiving, and moving off the ball exercise. I want to work with passing this week, so I will use the Hunt for the Funky Chicken exercise at the end of my session for fun and find two games I can edit to work with my Funky Chicken Island theme. For example, I want passing games, so Stuck in the Mud is now Stuck in the Sand, and Relay Passing is now Cross the Rickety Old Bridge. This is my session with a story going all the way through from start to end. As they play the games, I will have their full attention and will easily be able to coach them the correct technique (which is my goal for the session), selecting a few key points and sticking to them throughout all of the games.

Taking all this in mind, I ask you to do the same. Think of a story you like, whether it is a movie, book, or game you truly enjoy, and create a session around that idea. Give games different names to let their imaginations run wild and, most of all, have fun doing so! Enjoy being the focal point and love the hour you have with them. Tell your family and friends what you have created and the fun you had with the children you coach.

The idea of scrimmaging at the end of every practice is to give the kids a release from the learning and to have fun. This becomes very much apparent when the session is boring! If the sessions are fun, and there are entertaining activities where the players learn more about the game, why not continue those activities instead? If you have coached a U4–U7 team for a while in the old format of scrimmaging at the end of every session, then they will always ask for the scrimmage at the beginning. However, once you start with my style of coaching, by the second or third week, the kids want the end of the story more than a scrimmage. The more exciting we make the story or adventure, the more you as a coach want to finish the tale. This holds true for the players as well. The adventure should be their release from learning in the traditional sense. If we do this right, we can teach twice as much in this environment. In one season of eight practices, you can easily teach a MINIMUM of 20 skills and techniques (such as passing, shooting, shielding, and first touch). However, we are only touching on some of these techniques because the main focus should be individual brilliance. We want young players to be exposed to these techniques, but we need to put a larger emphasis on individual skill development. The ratio should be at least 70:30 skills to technique.

CHAPTER
SIX

SKILL BREAKDOWN: THE FOUNDATION FOR THE SESSIONS

SKILL BREAKDOWN: THE FOUNDATION FOR THE SESSIONS

Here is where the sessions begin. It can be a little difficult to read the skill descriptions below and put them into actions, but do not worry as you can do no wrong. If you are teaching the players to move with the ball in a certain way which is wrong as far as the terminology goes, you have still taught the players to flow with a ball. Who knows, you may have invented the best soccer skill known to man by accident and will become the most famous coach in the world. If this does actually happen, you can keep the fame and fortune if I get some of the credit. Perhaps name the skill after me? Just an idea.

These sessions contain a mixture of techniques and skills where most coaches, experienced or new, will not necessarily know the term for the action. Here is a complete breakdown of how to accomplish each skill related to the session the skill is used in.

PIRATE SHIP ADVENTURE

Action desired in the session	Actual name of the skill	How-to guide
Scrub the deck	Side to sides	Keep the upper body still and move the ball side to side between the feet, bending the knees on the spot.
Sweep the deck	Roll in, roll out	Roll the ball in with one foot; then after taking a step with the rolling foot, use that same foot to roll the ball out. After placing the foot back down on the floor, repeat the skill. Keep the body directly behind the ball at all times.
Mop the deck	Balance circles	Stand on one foot and move the ball around the standing leg, keeping that foot stuck on the floor (no hopping or twisting). Change direction and legs.
Dry the deck	Inside and outside cuts	With the same foot and without moving forward or backward, cut the ball with the inside, then the outside of the same foot, taking one step in between with the kicking foot.
Stormy sea	Sole rolls	Face the body 90 degrees from the direction of travel and drag the ball with the trailing leg, using the sole of the foot only. Every time the foot is lifted, there should be a roll of the ball with that foot.
Climb the rigging	Toe taps	Tap the ball with the left sole of the cleats then right as fast as possible, keeping the upper body as still as possible and trying to keep your eyes off the ball.

BIRTHDAY PARTY

Action desired in the session	Actual name of the skill	How-to guide
Dinner time and relay race	Speed dribbling technique	Point the toe down and inward slightly, with lots of quick touches directly forward using the outside of the same foot and keeping the head up.

OPERATION TAKE DOWN T-REX

Action desired in the session	Actual name of the skill	How-to guide
Stepoversaurus	Step over	Step over the ball and place this foot (e.g., right foot) directly in front of the standing foot. With the same foot, cut the ball using the outside of the foot.
Scissorsaurus	Scissors	Move feet in the opposite direction around the ball to the step over (feet shoulder-width apart, then move the foot inside initially, almost clicking heels. Then the foot moves around the ball inside to outside and then the foot returns to starting position). Foot moves all the way around the ball and returns to original position. The other foot starts another scissor, but instead of the foot going around the ball, the outside of the foot cuts the ball away (e.g., fake left, move right).
Cruyffysaurus	Cruyff	Put standing foot ahead of the ball. Play the ball with the other foot behind the standing leg, using the instep.

Action desired in the session	Actual name of the skill	How-to guide
Mathewsaurus	Mathews	Perform an inside cut, followed by an outside cut, taking one step with the kicking foot in between (i.e., inside and outside cuts moving forward).
Cristianosaurus	Cristiano	Initially both feet are behind the ball. Then simultaneously place the standing heel directly over the ball with the toe pointing out as far as possible and point the kicking foot out in the opposite direction, using the standing foot and the heel of this foot to kick the ball.
Shufflesaurus	Shuffle	Similar to the scissors, except the foot is not required to go around the ball. The body moves in a similar fashion, but now lunge the foot out to the side behind the ball. The kicking foot works in the same manner as in the scissors.

KNIGHTS OF THE ROUND TABLE

Action desired in the session	Actual name of the skill	How-to guide
Archers at the ready and battle for the maiden	Shooting technique	Point the toe down to the ground and lock the ankle of the kicking foot. The standing foot needs to be beside the ball with a little separation, and the toe of the standing foot points toward the target. Strike hard through the center of the ball and follow through by pointing the kicking foot at the target. (There are many more points to shooting, but keep it simple for now and focus on these few first.) Add rotation of the hips by approaching at an angle and landing on the kicking foot after impact.

DRIVING SCHOOL

Action desired in the session	Actual name of the skill	How-to guide
Red light	Stop	Place the sole of your foot on the ball and stop the ball from moving.
Reverse	Backward toe taps	Tap the ball with the left sole of the cleats then right as fast as possible, keeping the upper body as still as possible and trying to keep your eyes off the ball. Move backward slightly as the skill is continued.
	Backward side to side	Keeping the upper body still, move the ball side to side between the feet, bending the knees on the spot. Move backward slightly as the skill is continued.

Action desired in the session	Actual name of the skill	How-to guide
Left turn	Inside cut	Use the inside of the foot to change the direction of the ball, kicking the ball in a chopping, cutting motion with the heel down and toe pointed up. Preferably move your body outside the direction of the ball and fall into the ball and the turn.
	Outside cut	Reach out for the ball with the cutting foot, and in a chopping, cutting motion with the toe pointed up, cut the ball inward. Ensure the next step with the non-kicking foot blocks off the opponent and gives a good basis for acceleration.
Right turn	Inside cut	Same as above, using the right foot
	Outside cut	Same as above, using the right foot
Windshield wipers	Continuous scissor motion	Move feet in the opposite direction around the ball to the step over (feet shoulder-width apart, then move the foot inside initially, almost clicking heels. Then the foot moves around the ball inside to out and then returns to starting position). Move the foot all the way around the ball and return to the original position. The other foot starts the next scissor and repeats the action without moving the ball.
Emergency break turn	Drag back turn	Place heel on the ball, roll the ball back, and turn in to the ball.

Action desired in the session	Actual name of the skill	How-to guide
U-turn	U-turn	Stand outside the line of the ball, put your farthest foot on top of the ball, and roll the ball past the outside the standing foot directly backward. Turn promptly in the direction the ball is rolling.
Drifting	Inside cut circles	While attempting to stay on the same spot with your standing leg, use the inside of the foot to change the direction of the ball, kicking the ball in a chopping, cutting motion with the heel down and toe pointed up. Repeat several times, creating a tight circle around the standing leg.
	Outside cut circles	While attempting to stay on the same spot with your standing leg, reach out for the ball with the cutting foot and in a chopping, cutting motion with the heel down and toe pointed up, cut the ball inward several times creating a tight circle around the standing leg.
Yellow light	Outside of the foot close dribbles	Point the toe down and inward slightly and make lots of quick touches directly forward with the outside of the same foot, keeping the head up. Move the feet fast, but also move slowly forward.
Blue light	Speed dribbling	Point the toe down and inward slightly, make lots of quick touches directly forward with the outside of the same foot, keeping the head up. Move forward faster this time.

Action desired in the session	Actual name of the skill	How-to guide
Black light	Scoop	Put your toe underneath the ball and push the foot through the ball, scooping the ball in the air.
Purple light	Cruyff	Standing foot is ahead of the ball. Use the other foot to play the ball with the instep behind the standing leg.
White light	Mathews	Perform an inside cut, followed by an outside cut, taking one step with the kicking foot in between (e.g., inside and outside cuts moving forward).
Orange light	Shuffle	Similar to the scissors, except the foot is not required to go around the ball. The body moves in a similar fashion, but the foot now is lunged out to the side behind the ball. The kicking foot works in the same manner as in the scissors.

FUNKY CHICKEN ISLAND ADVENTURE

Action desired in the session	Actual name of the skill	How-to guide
Stuck in the sand, Crossing the rickety old bridge	Passing technique	With the standing foot level with the ball and pointing to the target, push the ball with the inside of the foot toward the target. Make sure the inside of the foot is presented to the target with the follow-through.

ALIEN INVASION

Action desired in the session	Actual name of the skill	How-to guide
Invisibility	Balance circles	Stand on one foot and move the ball around the standing leg, keeping that foot stuck on the ground (no hopping or twisting). Change direction and legs.
Open doors	Side to side	Keeping the upper body still, move the ball side to side between the feet, bending the knees on the spot.
Climb up the ladder	Toe taps	Tap the ball with the left sole of the cleats and then right as fast as possible, keeping the upper body as still as possible and trying to keep your eyes off the ball.
Shoot the lazers	Pull push	Pull the ball back with the sole of the foot, then push the ball out with the same foot using the laces. Then catch with the opposite foot and repeat with this foot.
Walking up the windy ramp	Inside cut circles	Use the inside of the foot to change the direction of the ball, kicking the ball in a chopping, cutting motion with the heel down and toe pointed up. Preferably move your body outside the direction of the ball and fall into the ball and the turn. Repeat continuously and turn in tight.

UNDER THE SEA ADVENTURE

Action desired in the session	Actual name of the skill	How-to guide
Shark defense	Forward push stop	Push the ball forward with the laces, and staying connected with the ball, move your foot up the ball and stop the ball rolling with the sole of your foot.
Octopus defense	No-touch step over	Swing your leg over the ball in the opposite direction to scissors. Start with your feet open. Push one foot forward and then around the ball. After this, put your foot down and take three quick steps before repeating with the other foot.
Piranha defense	Triangle	Pull the ball back with the sole of the foot, then pass the ball with the instep of the same foot toward the standing foot (left); then with that foot (left), pass the ball out to its original spot and stop the ball with the sole of the starting foot and repeat.
Stingray defense	L behind	Pull the ball back with the sole of the foot, then with the instep of the same foot pass the ball behind the standing foot. Turn toward the ball, then catch it with the sole of the standing foot and repeat. Take one step in between.
Killer whale defense	Roll-over stop	Place your foot on top of the ball and roll the ball in toward the standing foot and stop it with the inside of the standing foot. Then repeat.

CHAPTER
SEVEN

8-WEEK USEABLE PROGRAM WITH A HOW-TO GUIDE

8-WEEK USEABLE PROGRAM WITH A HOW-TO GUIDE

When you are on the field, the most important aspect in gaining control over a few or many players is tempo. If the majority of players are engaged, the rest will follow, so do not waste time corralling players to where you need them to be if this is not necessary. I would instead use a few techniques, which have been tried and tested through the years, to engage all the players and gain their attention.

KEY TECHNIQUES TO GAIN ATTENTION AND REINSERT FOCUS:

» **Clapping technique:** As a coach, say "If you can hear me, clap once. If you can hear me, clap twice," and if you need to, keep working up the claps until you gain full attention. The clap is a loud attention seeker, and a young player will be interested in what is happening and will join in when they realize they are left out of the clapping. Obviously wait for the clap before starting the next sentence, and clap along with the players.

» **Body parts technique:** As a coach, say "Everyone put your hands on your knees. Now touch your shoulders.....now put your hands on your mouth." This works similar to the clapping technique but is more visual rather than sound related. Name body parts at a relatively high tempo and end with hands on the mouth to ensure the talking will stop as you begin with your coaching point.

» **Movement technique:** As a coach, dribble your soccer ball to a corner and ask all the players to come follow as quick as they can. Move from corner to corner until all the players are engaged in movement, then stop and wait for all players to join you. I use this technique more than the other two because we want to keep the players active, and if a player

is shy or not really taking part with the session as much as
we like, I can move the herd of players to them.

In a normal session, I would arrive at the field and make sure I am completely set up 15 minutes prior to the start time. I believe it is important to captivate the player's imagination as soon as possible. When we see something a little interesting, our attention is immediately grasped and our intrigue is stirred. So I try to make the area look colorful, neat, and organized to give players a sense of enjoyment the moment they arrive. This does not mean that each week we will have crazy set-ups; in fact, it means quite the opposite. We want the boys and girls to understand the basic boundaries of our playing area so we do not have players running all over the complex; therefore, our boundary is definite. I would suggest using a cone every 4-6 yards instead of the recommended 8-10 at older ages because peripheral vision has not become fully developed as yet. As far as dimensions, I would operate in an area no larger than half of a game field the team is used to playing on, increasing the size of the field per every 2 teams (2 teams: half a field, 4 teams: full field, 6 teams: 1 ½ fields, etc.).

Once players arrive, I always look to revisit the skills and techniques worked on the previous session. I strongly dislike players arriving and shooting on the goal because this is a bad habit for players to pick up. Later in their career and when the muscle fibers are not ready for impact and aggressive stretching, shooting can easily pull muscles if the players have not completed a full warm-up. Instead we want the players to arrive ready to add to what they have learned as they refresh their memories. A good idea is to ask players if they remember the skills and games from the previous session.

To begin each practice, I want everyone to pay attention to the story and adventure we are about to begin. However, there are multiple factors we need to account for: weather, current conversations, other distractions, disengaging the players from their parents, and so on. To conquer all of these issues and more, I always begin with the movement technique. I do this for a minute until all players are running and focused on me before taking them into a corner. Make sure this corner has minimal distractions and that the sun will not be in the players' eyes. Once there, I instruct players to sit on their balls. Many coaches at the older ages instruct their players to never do this because the balls may lose their shape a little, which I agree with. I, however, would much rather teach players out of this habit at an older age than have to fight through players moving and playing with the balls while I am trying to talk. The less distractions the better! (Plus with players weighing 20 lbs, the balls should be ok.)

Once all players are sitting with me and before we engage the players with the story, I remind them of the ground rules. It is much better to police the players at the beginning rather than during the session. Lay down the law early, and express your expectations from the start.

THE GROUND RULES ARE:

» **Stay inside the cones:** Identify the boundary of the session and let the players know they are not permitted to leave the area. In some instances where the story includes a boundary, such as an island, we can relate to the boundary in this regard, and so we do not have to make the rules any more tedious than they have to be.

» **Bad hands, good feet:** We slap our hands twice and say "bad hands," and then we tap our feet twice and say "good feet." We repeat this faster and faster to make the rule fun, making sure no player uses their hands unless instructed to do so. We get the players to enforce the rule by encouraging them to show others the "bad hands, good feet" dance.

» **Good toes, naughty toes:** We ask every player to point their toes down and say "good toes," and then we ask the players to lift their toes up and say "naughty toes." We repeat saying "good toes, naughty toes, good toes, naughty toes..." as players move their toes into a good, downward pointing direction and then into the naughty, upward pointing direction. We then instruct players to never use their toes and to use their laces instead. Do not assume all the players know what laces are yet, so make all the players touch their laces so you can see what surface the player is considering to use.

» **It's nice to be nice:** Respect each other as to not push or hurt another player while we play. We are here to teach young people how to act in a group setting while being active and competitive, so make sure we do not take this responsibility lightly.

These ground rules, if enforced, will become ingrained into each player, and you will spend less time each week delivering the message on what you expect from them. From here you can coach the story you are about to tell.

A.   PIRATE SHIP ADVENTURE

The time you have been waiting for, potentially with a little bit of nerves and perhaps skepticism, is finally here. Take a deep breath and trust me when I say you are about to have a blast! As we are about to go on the Pirate Ship Adventure, prepare yourself to get into your first character, the captain of our fearless crew of pirates. Remember, the more you get into character, the more fun you, the players, the parents, and all involved will have. If you cannot control the urge to dress as a pirate, go for it, but this is not a requirement. Just remember to have fun with it and it's ok to be a kid every now and then.

After we have arrived early and set up the playing area, we are ready to engage the players. Attempt to create a fun and comfortable environment for the new players who you will be meeting for the first time. Allow them to speak and finish their sentences, regardless of what they are trying to tell you or how long it takes them to get the sentence out. This allows the players to open up to you, and they are showing their trust in you by discussing their thoughts, so do not shut them out.

The time for the session is here, Captain, so raise the energy and attentiveness by running to a corner and asking the pirates to follow (the movement technique). Move from corner to corner over and over until all of the pirates are with you and the session is ready to start. Move to a corner with the least distractions behind you, including sunlight, as you need all of their attention on you without squinting or players looking over your shoulder. From here, we need to begin telling the story. First, open up the floor to the players by asking, "Who would like to go on an adventure today?" Then, "What kind of adventure would you like to go on?" Make sure they raise their hands if they have an idea for the adventure, otherwise you may get more than you bargained for. You may need to guide their thoughts slightly, but for the most part the active imagination of a young person should be enough for the players to have some great suggestions. Use this time to plan future weekly topics as we are here to give the audience what they want when at all possible. We then let the pirates know we are going on a pirate ship adventure. We describe the session story to the pirates, letting them know we need to find the treasure, or "booty" (the kids will love saying booty).

Before we can find the treasure, we must dribble through the dangerous beach and sail across dangerous waters with other pirates and big sea creatures, all ready to attack our big pirate ship. Ask our pirates if they are ready for a pirate adventure, and if they are ready, they must make a hook with a finger, put one foot on the ball, close one eye, and say, "Aaaaargh!" Ask the pirates to make this gesture whenever you wish throughout the session to raise excitement or to regain attention. This works a lot better than asking a player to focus.

Here is where we can set the ground rules, letting the pirates know the playing area and why we need to stay inside the cones. Most pirates will realize that if we leave the pirate ship we will fall into the ocean where the scary sea creatures live, but we may need to let them know this is the reason why we need to stay inside of the coned area.

We then ask all the pirates to hold out their hands, and we ask, '"What are these?" We then say, "These are bad hands," as we slap our hands in time with the words. We then point to our feet and say, "What are these?" We then say, "Good feet," as we pat our feet in time with the words. Then we say, "Bad hands, good feet..." faster and faster until they cannot keep up.

Next we point our toes in the air and ask, "What are these?" We then say, "Naughty Toes." Then we point our toes to the ground and ask, "What are these?" Respond with, "Good toes." Now we raise our toes up and down repeating, "Good toes, naughty toes, good toes, naughty toes" with the actions.

Lastly, we remind our feisty pirates that it is nice to be nice, so no touching other players or playing too rough.

By now we have been talking for a few minutes and we are ready to play. Week 1 will always take longer with the explanations as players are not accustomed to the ground rules as of yet. Future weeks will become faster, especially when the experience the players are gaining improves.

Part 1: The adventure begins with the captain describing how the other pirates on our ship had a party last night, and we must clean up their mess before the ship is safe to set sail. First, we show the pirates how to scrub the deck by asking all the pirates to stand up and follow you. Once the pirates are slightly spread out (realistically this should happen in around 5 seconds), ask them to freeze and show the pirates how to "scrub the deck." These are side to sides, described in the previous chapter. Once they have a basic understanding of what they need to do, point to areas of the ship that need scrubbing and ask them to help scrub each area. Here is where you or any assistants you may have can attend to those players who are not grasping the technique while the other players are gaining valuable repetitions. After a few minutes of practice on this skill, move to sweeping the deck, mopping the deck, and drying the deck, using the same method as described. Once all skills are mastered for the most part, give the pirates 2 minutes to clean the deck, using all four techniques as fast as they can. Point to new areas to spread the pirates out and ask for specific skills during this time as they clean. Do not stop the group during this period. Instead, let them work to the best of we loosen the reins. Do not worry about taking above the 15 minutes allotted to learn these skills as they are important and what the session is all about. Once they have completed cleaning the deck, send the pirates for a quick water break.

Part 2 of the adventure begins with the movement technique once more to quickly bring all the pirates back from their break. Move to a corner and ask pirates to sit on their soccer balls again as we describe the second part of the story. We may need to use another technique to gain attention because the energy and excitement levels are high. Describe how we are setting sail, looking out for the island where we buried our treasure. Generally as a rule we do not want to talk for long unless absolutely necessary, so ask the pirates to follow you as you sail around the ocean. After the pirates have followed you around the square for a short while, inform them that the sea is a little rough, and the ship is swaying from side to side. Be in front of the pirates and point to the direction we are rolling and ask them to roll their foot over the ball in this direction with you, sway the other way, and repeat. You will need to stop the pirates and teach them the correct technique as many players will use their right foot when moving to the right which is incorrect. They need to drag the ball along with their back foot, rolling this foot over the top of the ball every time they lift it in the air. Once they grasp this technique, move to smoother seas, and dribble as normal. Move into rough seas a few times to see if they can remember the skill of sole rolls before asking the pirates to climb to the top of the ship so we can get to the lookout point. Use toe taps and move arms as if on a ladder. Many players will not touch the top of the ball every time, and you will need to insist on perfection before speed, using the ladder analogy: Ask what would happen if we did not step on each rung of the ladder? This should help most players use the correct technique. Try to not slow the session down by ensuring every player is perfect, but coach these players while the other pirates are pushing themselves. See who can climb the fastest, and once we are at the top of the ship, ask each pirate to get their telescopes out and look for the island. Pirates will say they can see the island, but look for pirates with their hands up when you ask them a question (we are trying to instill manners as well as coach). Ask the pirates if they can see the island and when they point in a direction say, "That's not the island, it's a killer whale!!" Run away and ask the boys and girls to do the same with the volume and intensity you would expect if you did see a killer whale. The more enthusiastic and realistic you and the pirates are, the more fun you all will have. Do this several times as we spot multiple creatures, such as an octopus, a giant squid, sharks, piranhas... until we see a pirate ship.

If you have assistants, make them become the bad pirates. Tell the players how their magic soccer balls are now soccer swords and tell them to take down the bad pirates by kicking their soccer balls against the bad pirates' legs, chopping them off. After a few minutes, tell the pirates that they have taken down all of the bad pirates, but the scariest pirate of all time, Blackbeard (or a different color if you can attach a pinny or bib to your face, and becoming Bluebeard, for instance) has boarded the ship. This will be you, so now all the pirates will be after you, attempting to hit balls against your legs. If you have no assistants, then start at this point. Try and make your demise as dramatic as possible, losing legs as you hop, then on your knees until you are lying on the ground with kids firing balls at you. Sit up quickly and celebrate how the pirates all killed Blackbeard, and we have reached the island. From here, send the pirates for a water break. This part of the session may take a little longer than the 15 minutes also, but do not worry, the next two stages are relatively quick in comparison.

Part 3 brings us to Crabby Beach. Ask all the pirates to follow you once more using the movement technique and bring all pirates to one end of the field. Ask all pirates to leave their balls on the cone line and to come with you to the middle of the area. Tell the pirates how our soccer balls are on the ship, but we need to get them across the beach and onto the island at the other side of the grid where the treasure and other booty is hidden. Tell the pirates how the beach is dangerous because giant crabs are all around, trying to kick the soccer balls away from you as they try and keep you off of the island. Once explained, ask all the pirates to spread out around the entire square and sit on the ground. You may have to demonstrate the crab position by sitting down and then elevating your body with your hands and feet on the ground. Once every pirate can get themselves into the crab position, ask for a few pirates to go to their balls and wait to begin, preferably using approximately a quarter to a third of the total number of participants. Generate excitement by asking the pirates if they are ready. If they are, ask them to close one eye, make a finger hook, and say, "Aaaaargh!!" Then ask the crabs if they are ready, and if they are, ask them to pinch their claws together and make a sound of your choice (I generally ask for a clicking noise for their claws clicking together). Once everyone is ready, say, "Go!" Police the crabs, making sure they stay in the crabby position throughout. After the first group of pirates reaches the end, ask them to leave their balls and rejoin the crabs as you select the next group to go. From here, we can coach the players to keep the ball closer to them using their ball mastery skills, such as the sole rolls and the inside and outside cuts to change direction. Once all the pirates have gotten their soccer balls across, celebrate with all the pirates before sending them away for a water break. A good ole fashioned pirate jig and song is always a winner.

Part 4: The Finale. Here we have found the treasure, but we have to find a way to get the booty back to the ship. The game itself can have multiple variations, but as the game is not on the topic of ball mastery, we are using this set-up to allow the players to have fun and a release from coaching for us. This is the time to be quiet and allow the pirates to have fun as they compete. The game written in the session is a difficult version, aimed toward high-level U8 players, but there are multiple, easier variations for the game. The easiest would be to separate the players equally with the number of coaches there are. If you are on your own then there will be one group. Have all the balls at one end of the playing area and have one goal at the other end representing the Pirate Ship. To score the treasure, pirates must pass the ball to every pirate in their team before we can score. As young players are very protective of their own balls, make sure they come and get their own ball to start the passing sequence, and then they receive their ball at the end of the passing sequence to score that piece of treasure. Repeat until all the balls are in the goal and every pirate gets to score. If there are two or more teams, see what team can score all their treasure first to add a competitive aspect to the game. With no defenders, this should be a lot easier, and every pirate will have the opportunity to be the hero and score, regardless of ability. Some pirates may slow the process down as they are new soccer players, but be patient and guide them to the best of your ability.

The session is over, so you want to bring the pirates in to you one last time. Here we wish to remind the pirates of all the skills they have accomplished and that you wish to see every skill performed in the game they are to have next. We also want each pirate to leave knowing how much fun they have had, so make this loud and exciting.

Ask the pirates initially what we did on our adventure in sequential order. Whenever they talk about a part of the adventure where we taught skill, ask the pirate if they can remember how to "scrub the deck" or "sweep the deck," and ask all of the pirates to show you the skills. Go over the session until all aspects and skills of the session are discussed and revisited. Ask the pirates if they had fun over and over until they are shouting out loud, then I generally ask the players to shout, "We love soccer!" before saying they can leave and to not forget their soccer ball, water bottles, and any trash they may have left behind. If you wish to ask the pirates to help you with the cones, feel free to do so!

Now is the time to be a captain for all involved in your soccer program. This could, perhaps be the most important conversation of your soccer season; you must educate the other coaches and parents on what to expect this season and beyond. Inform all people involved how you are looking to develop each player individually and how the sessions will accomplish this goal. More importantly, educate everyone on the support you need during the games. You will be pleasantly surprised that most, if not all, parents and coaches will want the players to become technically great, and they care little about scoring goals at this age. Ideas on exactly what to do on the game days is discussed toward the end of the book, so sit tight. If you are mentoring coaches through the program, break down the session to them, and explain how the session flows, teaching and progressing the ball mastery skills throughout the story. The more you include every parent, player, and coach involved, the better support you will receive. If any push back is given by any person, ask them to be patient and give it a try first. If you help them understand what you are doing, people are generally receptive to this and will come around. If you are not understanding of their concerns, you will build a wall which may be wide enough for them to never come around. Sometimes change is hard, but for the most part you should not have any issues.

SESSION TOPIC	KEY COACHING POINTS
Pirate Ship (Ball mastery)	1. Use the correct technique 2. Fast feet 3. Head up

Session Story: All the players are pirates on the pirate ship in the search for treasure. Their ball is their sword as we go on an adventure, fighting pirates and sailing to islands along the way. The coach is the fearless captain of the ship in charge of all his or her crew.

PIRATE SHIP PARTY CLEAN-UP OPERATION

Each player has a ball and moves throughout the area, cleaning up the mess which was left from the party. Using the ball, the players are to scrub the deck with side to sides, sweep the deck with roll in, roll outs. Create whatever duties can be performed to teach ball mastery skills.

PIRATE SHIP PARTY CLEAN-UP OPERATION

www.sports-graphics.com

Coaching points: 1. Use the correct technique

2. Fast feet

3. Head up

PIRATE ATTACK

Players climb the mast by performing toe taps and looking for approaching pirates. Do this a few times before the pirates are spotted and they come on board. From there, the players use their swords (the balls) to hit each other's swords before fighting Blackbeard the Pirate (the coach).

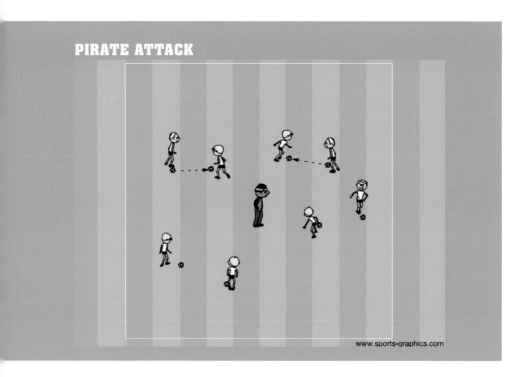

PIRATE ATTACK

www.sports-graphics.com

Coaching points: 1. Use the correct technique

2. Fast feet

3. Head up

CRAB DODGING

All the players except one lie down on their backs and then use their arms and legs to elevate their bodies into the crab position. Once ready, the player who is waiting on one side of the square attempts to travel through the crabs to the other side without the crabs kicking the ball away into the water outside the square. Every player has at least one turn each, and if they are younger players, have two players attempt to get past the crabs at one time.

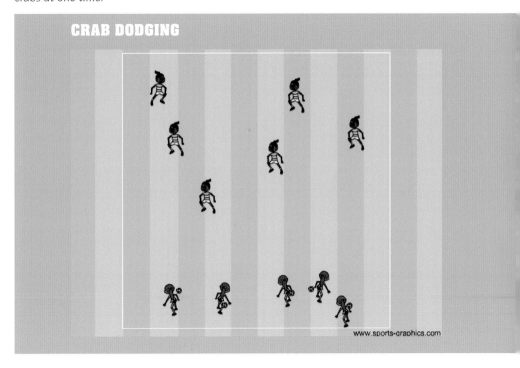

CRAB DODGING

www.sports-graphics.com

Coaching points: 1. Close control
2. Fast feet
3. Head up

KEEP THE TREASURE

Divide the players into two equal teams and establish a playing area roughly half the size of the field. Have the players spread out all over the playing area. Toss the ball in to start. The goal is to gain control of the ball and make three passes in a row between teammates. If the defense intercepts, then that team tries to make three passes in a row. After a score of three successful passes, the coach restarts with a ball thrown in. Play for a certain duration of time, or until 10 points are scored.

KEEP THE TREASURE

www.sports-graphics.com

Coaching points: 1. Spread out

2. Quick passes

3. Make good decisions

B.   BIRTHDAY PARTY

What a day! Coach, it has been a long time coming, but it's your birthday! It is time to celebrate with your players and have a good time in soccer. Throughout the session the players are to do whatever the coach wants and play the coach's favorite games. The session is designed to work on speed dribbling, so any game that has the speed dribbling aspects involved, feel free to stop them and demonstrate the speed dribbling technique, found in chapter 6.

You will see as the session continues, this session has been strategically placed for organizations to force coach interaction with their players. Whoever is hosting the session will always need help from the coaches, and this session ensures this will happen. If not, this session can be a disaster, so prepare the coaches to get their hands dirty, and you will do just fine.

Part 1: Using the corner running technique, get the players active and ready to play. After a minute or so, take them to a corner out of the sun so we do not blind the players and ask them what adventure they want to go on today. Let their imaginations run wild until telling them it is the Coach's Birthday Adventure. Ask the players what they normally do on their birthday before telling them how hungry you are. Ask them where they would like to eat for their birthday and go to the corner of your square to the restaurant. Act as the waiter and ask the kids which food items they wish and serve them their imaginary food. Everyone scarfs the food down and then ask the kids where to go next. Feel free to dictate a restaurant every now and then; it is your birthday after all. Make sure between corners the players are dribbling correctly with no "naughty toes." After about 10 minutes of "feeding" their imaginations, send the players for a water break as we set up the next part of the session.

Part 2: The next part of the session is "coach in the middle." This gives an opportunity for the players to get visual recognition of the field to strengthen their decision making. A version of this game is used in the professional game for warm-up, so players can gain this experience at a young age with your help.

Separate the players into groups. Generally each team will have no more than eight players at this age, and this number is about the largest we would prefer. If you are dealing with multiple coaches and teams, ask each coach to take their teams and play the game between their own players. Have the coach in the middle and create a circle around the coach with the players. Ensure the players are not too far away from each other, so have the radius of the circle no bigger than 5 yards (4.5 meters). Have the coach in the middle and one ball between all of the players. The players attempt to keep possession of the ball away from the coach by looking at their teammates and passing to them, using either their laces (preferred for this session) or the inside of their feet. The lead coach will need to be free from a team to instruct the coaches. As a coach, understand that we are looking for success, so do not challenge a player for the ball. Instead, block off some of the passing options by standing to one side of the player with the ball. We will coach the player to pass away from the defender. For advanced players, ask them to call out the player's name they are attempting to pass the ball toward. This will improve player communication and stop the coach (us) from talking too much. We want to give the game to the players and allow them to express themselves. The more we talk, the less opportunity they have to speak themselves. After doing this for a while, you may allow players to become the coach in the middle. Instruct them to not challenge the player on the ball, but they can intercept the pass. Once all of the players have had success, send them for a water break.

As you can see in the last exercise, all coaches must step up and take charge. The lead coach is becoming more of a coach instructor throughout the session rather than the coach of multiple teams. This is where we are really putting the responsibility onto the coaches to develop their team. This next part of the session is no exception as we direct the focus back to the session topic of speed dribbling.

Part 3: The under-over relay race is played with multiple lines of players who are lined up one behind each other. We as coaches should never be a fan of lines whereas players are waiting to play while other players are engaged. In this exercise, the line is part of the exercise, so this is acceptable. **PLEASE TRY TO AVOID LINES IN SESSIONS YOU WISH TO CREATE UNLESS PLAYERS ARE ACTIVE IN THEIR LINE.** For the set-up, have the same amount of lines as you have coaches, and insert the coach as part of the line.

Give them the flexibility to leave their place in line to assist their team. By inserting the coach, we will add tempo and engage the coach even further in the session. To start the game, the coach will pick up the ball and pass the ball to the player behind them by holding the ball behind their head. The next player would take the ball and give it to the player behind them by holding the ball between their legs. This is repeated until the ball has traveled to the last person in line who would then drop the ball, and speed dribble to a cone, 10 yards (9 meters) ahead, round the cone, and join the front of the line. This player would then pick up the ball, and the process is repeated. As the lead coach, ensure the coaches of each team are supporting the ball by running with the players and communicating to each player to correct mistakes rather than telling them what to do. Guide the players, do not control them. Once the whole team has completed the task, the players need to sit down in their line and have the ball at the front of the line for them to win. Play a few times and coach the dribbling technique. A slalom of cones can be used for higher-level players, but do not place them too close. We are looking for speed, not precision in this session. If you have differing levels of abilities between lines, feel free to create a slalom for the elite-level players and not for the lower-level players. Also if there is not an even number of players in each line, make the first player go twice in the lines with one less player.

Part 4: The last game is a release, which is still using the laces, as we stay on a similar topic. Kickball can last for a long time, but we do need to ensure every player gets an opportunity to shine. The set-up is similar to baseball as we have a batter (kicker), pitcher, and the bases. With the coach as the pitcher, we separate the players into two teams. One team is fielding, so they spread themselves around the field, while the other is at bat, and they line up waiting for their turn. Again, we do not like lines, so try and move the game along quickly. The pitcher rolls the ball slowly toward the kicker and he or she kicks the ball with the laces away from the fielders. For the player to score, the player must run around the bases and make it home before the ball gets back to the coach. The coach is not allowed to move as the fielder must dribble the ball to the

pitcher's mound. The moment the ball is touched by the pitcher, the player is out. In the session there is an advanced variation which is pass-orientated rather than dribble-oriented, so choose the game you wish to play with your players. As the pitcher, it is imperative to keep the ball moving. Once every player has had a kick, change over teams and see who wins. This game can easily take a whole hour, so attempt to move the game along quickly. You may need to have two set-ups if there are a large number of players.

At the end of the session, bring the players in and ask them if they had fun. Get them screaming their responses as they exert their energy and excitement, while gaining their attention, and then ask the players to describe the technique of speed dribbling. Ask the players to help with clean-up and send them home for a good night's sleep after all this hard work.

Here is a great moment to thank the coaches for all their hard work. As you may know, a lot of work goes unappreciated when you are the coach, so reach out to your supporting cast and make sure you let them know how helpful they are being. Without them in a session like this, life will be extremely hard. Give credit early and make people feel needed, and they will support you throughout the season.

SESSION TOPIC	KEY COACHING POINTS
Coach's Birthday Party (Speed dribbling)	1. Push the ball forward with the laces 2. Stay connected with the ball at pace 3. Head up

Session Story: Yep, you guessed it! It's Coach's birthday, and we are playing all the games Coach wants to play and eating what Coach wants to eat on his special day. The kids are all here to enjoy his day with him.

DINNER TIME!

Coach is in need of some food to get his party started, but he wants something a little more special than crabby patties today. Ask the players what their favorite restaurant is and run as fast as you can with the ball to any area on the field and get the kids to follow. Once there, everyone can order something from the menu. Repeat this all over the field until all the kids have had their choice. Make sure a lot of distance is covered and enough down time at each restaurant is timed, but not too much down time.

DINNER TIME!

www.sports-graphics.com

Coaching points: 1. Push the ball forward with the laces

2. Stay connected with the ball at pace

3. Head up

COACH IN THE MIDDLE

Divide the kids into groups of four. Three players set up in a triangle with one ball leaving one coach in the middle. The three players in the triangle pass the ball around while the middle player tries to get it. If he gets it, the passing player goes into the middle as coach.

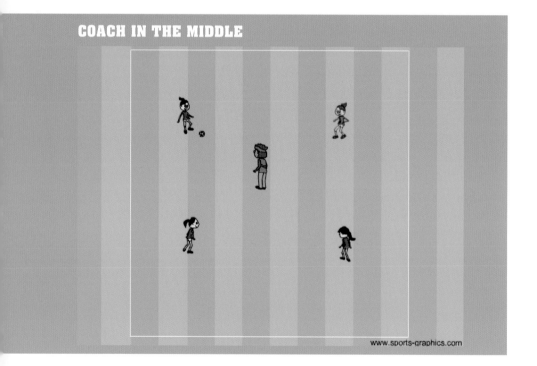

COACH IN THE MIDDLE

www.sports-graphics.com

Coaching points: 1. Push the ball forward with the laces

2. Stay connected with the ball at pace

3. Head up

UNDER-OVER RELAY RACE

Separate the players into two or three lines, depending on the amount of players you have. A cone is to be 20 yards ahead of each line. The ball starts at the front and is passed from player to player in the line until it reaches the player in the back. The ball is to be in the players' hands and is passed over the head to the second person, then through the legs to the third, then over to the fourth, etc. until the ball gets to the player at the back. The player then dribbles the ball around the top cone and to the front of the line where he picks the ball up and repeats the under-over. The team where every player completes the dribble first wins.

Coaching points: 1. Push the ball forward with the laces

                        2. Stay connected with the ball at pace

                        3. Head up

KICKBALL

Set this up like a kickball game, using cones to lay out the bases. All the players are in the field except for the player up to bat. The pitcher (the coach) passes the ball in, and the kicker kicks it as far as she or he can and starts to run the bases. She continues to circle the bases until all the players in the field have touched the ball. The field players must one-touch or trap the ball and pass to another field player until everyone has touched it, at which point the runner is out.

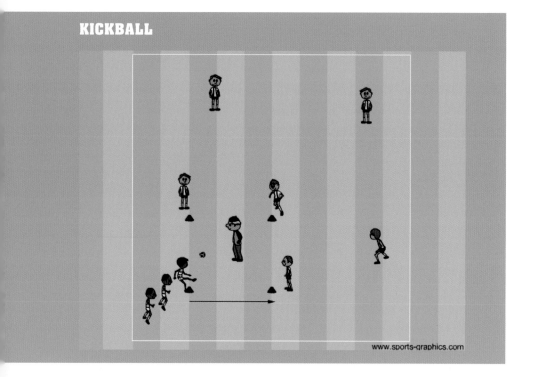

KICKBALL

www.sports-graphics.com

Coaching points: 1. Push the ball forward with the laces

2. Stay connected with the ball at pace

3. Head up

C. OPERATION TAKE DOWN T-REX

Ok cavemen and cavewomen, now is the time to show your real fighting skills and instincts. Today we are fighting against the deadliest creature to ever walk the earth. Be strong, as it is you who are here to protect the cave-kids and show the big bad dinosaur who's the boss. If you feel the need to dress up and really play the part of caveman or cavewoman, feel free, but this is not a requirement! The more you get into character, however, the more enjoyable any session will be for the cave-kids and for you.

Today's session involves the toughest, yet most rewarding skills in the program, so take a little time to perfect what they are doing when we get to the jungle run part of the session.

The session is about to begin, so start with the movement technique. Get all of the cave-kids engaged and go to the middle of the field in the lava (to be explained in a moment) where you are looking into the sun so the cave-kids don't have to. Go through the ground rules once more and let them guess what adventure we are going on today. Explain how we are on an adventure to take down T-Rex, but this will not be easy as we have to find T-Rex's lair, go through the jungle, and pass the huge, scary dinosaurs.

Part 1: First we travel back through time and land next to a volcano. Ask the cave-kids what happens when a volcano erupts, and when they speak about the lava, say, "Oh no!! We are in a river of lava; quickly get to the river banks!" Shepherd the cave-kids so equal numbers are on each side. This should help them to stay out of the lava, but you will spend most of this part of the session keeping the cave-kids out of the middle, but that's ok. Explain how their soccer balls have become dinosaur T-Rex eggs, and if they hatch, dinosaurs will come out and get them. Here is the time to work cavemen: Have you ever tried to take a soccer ball away from a young cave-kid? Good luck! No cave-kid wants to kick their ball away. Instead they would rather hold their ball like a teddy and sleep with it if they had the choice, so it's time to break the cave-kids like wild stallions! Or we can be really encouraging and tell them they desperately do not want to have a ball on their side of the lava river. Your choice (I strongly suggest the second option). Once you think the cave-kids understand, let the games begin. Cave-kids attempt to kick their ball across the lava to the team on the other side. Ask the other cavemen and cavewomen to either be in the lava to keep cave-kids out and to move balls that did not reach the other side of the river or to be on one side to encourage cave-kids who are not moving toward other balls on their side. After a few minutes, start a countdown and get every cave-kid to freeze when you call time. It is important to train the cave-kids early to stop when you say stop, so move any ball kicked after the time has ended to the other side before counting up to find the winner. The losing team is now standing in an area where the dinosaurs are hatching out of the balls, so make this fun and get them all to run away WITH YOU (we do not want young cave-kids running into other sessions) screaming and waving their hands in the air. (Losing can be fun if we want it to be.) Feel free to play again and make sure the other team wins. Let them have a quick water break from the waterfall and come back as we have someone very special to meet!

Part 2: Yep, it's you! You are the special caveperson (but you know that already). You are about to become a dinosaur! What a day! Initially when the cave-kids come back, let them know you are going to take them to meet some friendly dinosaurs who are to show you their secrets of hiding from the scary T-Rex. If they can do the dino-skills, they will freeze any dinosaur for a few seconds so the cave-kids can get away. Take them to the forest on the other side of the lava to meet one of the dinosaurs. This is

where the fun begins, cavemen! Maneuver your attire around and look crazy as you become a crazy dinosaur. Show the cave-kids your dino-skills. (In order of difficulty there are: Shufflesaurus, Matthewsaurus, Cruyffsaurus, Scissorsaurus, Stepoversaurus, and Cristianosaurus). I suggest selecting three of these skills, but do one at a time and ask the cave-kids to practice by approaching one of the dinosaurs and attempting to freeze them with their dino-skills. The funnier the freeze, the more the cave-kids will want to attempt the skills, so go crazy. When you are ready to coach the next skill, take the cave-kids to the other side of the jungle. Learning skills takes a little time and a little bit of standing around the same areas, so break up the monotony with a little run to the other side of the field. Once all three skills are taught, send the cave-kids away to get water from the river because they need to get their energy up to get through the jungle.

Part 3: Now the challenge begins, cave-people! You are about to take the kids to run through the jungle, but T-Rex is waiting for them. Can the cave-kids make it through the jungle safely? Of course they can with their crazy dino-skills! Set all the cave-kids up on one side of the jungle and get the dinosaurs to spread out. Tell the players they need to get through the T-Rex to the other side of the jungle, but they must freeze at least one T-Rex before making it through the jungle. This will encourage each cave-kid to attempt the skill. The cave-kids need to do this six times, two runs for each skill, and demand the specific skill you wish to see. If not, a cave-kid will use one skill only every time, which is limiting their success of skill development. Hopefully you will see through this session how even the youngest of players can develop skill in soccer. Once each player is through, send them away as they get ready to take down T-Rex!

Part 4: Caveman and cavewoman, it is time to get your cave-kids ready to fight the big T-Rex. With the goals in the middle of the field placed back to back and the dinosaurs protecting the cave, it is going to be hard for the players to shoot their soccer spears into the cave. If a dinosaur can get to a ball, they will kick or throw the ball away from the cave, but the cave-kids have a secret weapon: their dino-skills! If a player uses the skill correctly, the T-Rex will be frozen, allowing the cave-kid to score. If a cave-kid is to attempt a skill, allow them to succeed, but if a cave-kid is trying to score without freezing the dinosaur, let them pay. Every now and then, throw the spears out of the cave with a roar, like the big dinosaur you are, and keep the game going until you are ready for the session to end. Once all the spears are in the cave, the dinosaurs become dramatically extinct. Loud roars and an elaborate fall to the ground is always a classic way to go out; then you are back to being the tough caveperson once more.

Bring the cave-kids to a corner and conclude the session by going through their accomplishments. Ask players to show you their dino-skills and encourage them to use these skills in their game. Tell the players how, if they use their dino-skills in a game, they could one day be as good and brave like you!

Here is what I regard as the most important conversation with your coaches, for if the skills we teach are not utilized in the game, we have failed. However, it is hard to convince a coach to value skill development over winning. The hope is to generate an environment where skill is frequent enough to give us multiple coaching points on when, where, and how to use the skill correctly in a game environment. To create a setting where skill can flourish is tough, yet extremely rewarding. Hopefully the coaches will get to experience the greatest feeling in the world: To know you have given a player their moment of brilliance in soccer. Every player has the opportunity to be amazing; it is up to us to empower them to grow without restraint or fear of making a mistake.

SESSION TOPIC	KEY COACHING POINTS
Operation Take Down T-Rex (Moves 1v1)	1. Use the correct technique 2. Fast feet 3. Accelerate away

Session Story: Our soccer players have travelled back in time to the age of the dinosaurs. In this adventure, the soccer cave-kids are removing the dinosaur eggs before they hatch, learning soccer skills from the friendly dinosaurs all to try and beat the big T-Rex

REMOVE THE EGGS

Create a neutral area between the two teams where no player is allowed. This area can be as small as 1 yard and as big as 10 yards wide. The width is determined by how far the players can kick the ball. Each player starts with a ball at her or his feet. On command, each team tries to keep their side of the game zone free of balls by kicking their ball over to the other team's side.

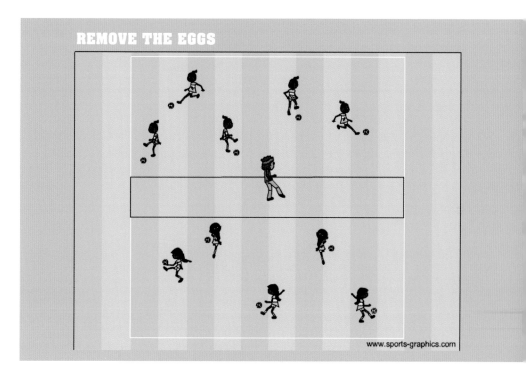

REMOVE THE EGGS

www.sports-graphics.com

Coaching points: 1. The standing foot is level with the ball
   and pointing at the target

2. Use the laces of the cleat with the toe
   pointed downward

3. Point the toes of the kicking foot to
   the target after impact

DINO-SKILLS

The kind dinosaurs would like to help us out on our mission, and they have offered to teach their skills to the kids. Hopefully with all the skills the cave-kids can go on to defeat the T-Rex! We will meet the Stepoversaurus, Scissorsaurus, Cruyffsaurus, Mathewsaurus, Cristianosaurus, and the Shufflesaurus and learn their secrets.

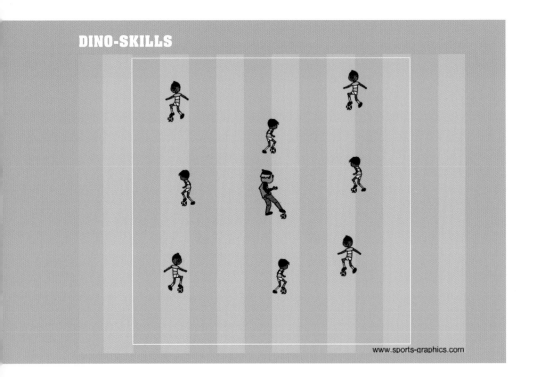

DINO-SKILLS

www.sports-graphics.com

Coaching points: 1. Use the correct technique

2. Fast feet

3. Accelerate away

JUNGLE RUN

When T-Rex hears about our mission, he comes to get us! We need to run away through the jungle to get away from the scary dinosaur. The path is narrow, so set up a narrow, running area in which all the players must stay. The players must make it past the T-Rex to the other side without being caught. If a player uses one of the dino-skills, then T-Rex is frozen and cannot get the cave-kid for 2 seconds.

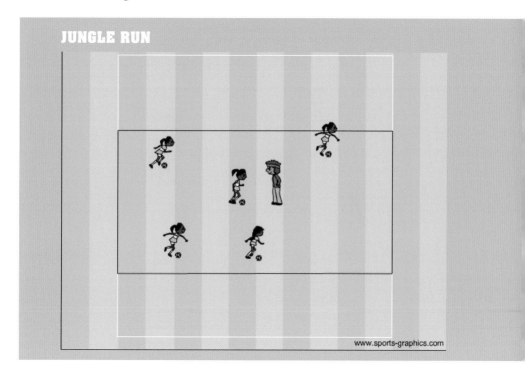

JUNGLE RUN

www.sports-graphics.com

Coaching points: 1. Use the correct technique

2. Fast feet

3. Accelerate away

TAKE DOWN T-REX

We have made it to T-Rex's lair, and it's time to take him down as a team. The lair is a collection of three goals back to back, and we need to shoot our soccer ball cave spears into the lair to win. If the T-Rex catches a ball, then he will throw it far away. The T-Rex will still freeze if a skill is used. When all the balls are in the goals, it's time to attack. The kids now use their balls as clubs and take down the T-Rex by kicking the soccer ball clubs at the dinosaur.

TAKE DOWN T-REX

www.sports-graphics.com

Coaching points: 1. Use the correct technique

2. Fast feet

3. Accelerate away

D.   KNIGHTS OF THE ROUND TABLE

We are going back in time to the age of knights and dragons. Fair maidens are waiting to be saved, so without further ado, let us get started my brave kings and queens!

The set-up for this session can create intrigue and wonder. As we are knights of the round table, the field will need to be round. This works initially as a boundary for players to stay outside because we are to set up towers and a castle made of cones, which with many eager and energetic knights can become very fragile and will easily fall over or be disturbed. There are two main ways to set up a tower: Either place two cones very close together and balance a third cone on top, or place a soccer ball on a cone. Either looks great and gives the players a target. Place the towers about 6 yards from the edge and have many towers surrounding the castle directly in the middle of the circle. This castle is a large tower, so place a few towers together to build your castle. As you can see, the set-up creates intrigue and wonder for our brave knights to imagine what fun they are about to encounter.

Our knights have many challenges today, and their equipment is pivotal to their survival against dragons and ice witches, so let's protect them with coats of armor. After the movement technique, describe the session and help our knights dress in armor, disguised as soccer pinnies. Make sure they are aware of the rules of "bad hands, good feet" and "naughty toes," especially with the shooting element about to take place. You may wish to get the players to stand up and do "good toes, naughty toes." This is where the players point their toes to the ground and say "good toes." Then the players point their toes up to the sky and say "naughty toes." Do this over and over to get their ankles moving and to remind players what position their foot should be in for practice. Allow the knights to guess what adventure we are about to experience and lead them back in time, setting the scene. Use your imagination to create excitement, talking about wizards, witches, queens, princesses, knights, and dragons. The more engaged in the story our knights are, the easier they will be to handle.

Part 1: The first part of the story begins the training to become knights of the round table. Initially the cones are targets as we are at the archery range to perfect their bow and arrow skills. Separate the players around the circle, making sure they are not

71

too close to a cone as many players at this age will not see the cone as an obstacle and will kick through the ball and the cone which will create inaccuracy and improper technique. Make the knights aware initially that they must shoot the arrow with their bow. Most players will have laces which they have tied in a "bow" (how convenient). Instruct the knights to use this part of their foot and that they cannot fire inside of the range as they could hit someone else with their arrow. Count the players down with a, "Ready, aim, FIRE!" and make sure each player is using the correct surface. Ask the players to return to their spot and go through the process once more with instruction on how to shoot properly in between.

Once we have practiced for a few minutes, it is time to free the princess or prince hidden in the tower and protected by the dragon. Girls may not want another girl around as they are daddy's princess, so that will be you, soldier (and the other coaches). Dragons can only stop arrows shot inside of the circle, so players can have free shots from outside. Encourage this as we want the players to shoot from range and get their heads up to see targets from far away. If a knight attempts to shoot their arrow inside of the circle, feel free to act as a dragon and fly their soccer ball away, or set it on fire with your breath (the first may be more effective unless you have not used tooth paste for a while). Once all the towers are broken and the castle has been demolished, send the knights in training for a water break.

Part 2: Bring the knights back and tell them how the Ice Witch has taken the beautiful damsel in distress and taken her to the Ice Maiden Cave. Now kings and queens, hopefully you are female or have a lady ready to be a witch in your group of coaches, or else you better practice your cackle! Make yourself pretty or at least somewhat lady-like by taking a pinnie and placing it on your head as a wig. Now remember, kings, you are not looking to win any drag queen awards as you are a wicked witch, so don't go all out trying to look cute; the hideous and scarier the better. Position yourselves at the far end of the circle and notify the knights that if they can do a great freeze with their foot on top of the ball, the wicked Ice Witch will not be able to see them, especially if the freeze looks funny. Let the knights know they cannot throw (or kick) their soccer ball swords at the Ice Witch; they must push their fiery sword into the Ice Witches leg for her to melt. Do not be afraid to work on your *Wizard of Oz* Wicked Witch of the West melting scene

as you act dramatically in the hope for a standing ovation from the parents. Play the game and turn frequently, pointing at knights to send back to the start if they move. Encourage them to push the ball forward with their laces with their toes pointed down. Once melted, send the knights for a deserved water break.

Part 3: In the words of the Highlander, "There can be only one." It is time for the battle royal to see who the bravest and strongest knight of them all is. Who will earn the right to save the beautiful princess? The knights are to take part in the biggest battle known to man as they fight one another. Their mission: to hit as many swords as they can. If they hit a sword and they make a loud "ching" sound with their mouths, they get a point. To score a point, they MUST hit the ball with their laces, and the knight with the most points will win. However, swords are dangerous, so there are rules to the battle. If a sword leaves the ground, points can be taken away, even disqualification from the battle may occur. If a sword hits a leg, then the leg is chopped off, but do not fear! There are wizards and good witches who are on hand to help. If you have a leg removed, hop to the nearest witch or wizard and give a healing high five to grow your leg back. If both legs are removed, crawling on their knees is perfectly acceptable. To define the coach as a wizard, I suggest growing beards by hooking the pinnie shoulder holsters over the ears.

Play the game, and halfway through, throw a spanner in the works. The evil Black Knight will enter the arena, ready to take on every knight for the rights to the princess. You guessed it, the Black Knight is you! Use your skill and wit to fight bravely–until they gang up on you and kick your butt... literally. As they pelt you with balls, lose your limbs dramatically until you are on the floor, crying out in pain as they relentlessly continue to stab and slice at your defenseless body. Sit up and congratulate the players for killing the Black Knight and send them for a water break. Hopefully there aren't too many bruises. Just remember you are a brave king or queen, and you can get through this, especially as the last part of the session gives you a little rest.

Part 4: It's a good news/bad news situation for our brave knights. The good news is they all defeated the Black Knight, so they all can save the princess or prince. The bad news is as everyone was fighting in the battle royal, a big, scary giant has taken the princess and is hiding her in his cave. The giant is big and scary, with huge legs, massive arms, giant teeth, a bald and shiny head, a spiky beard, and a big belly from eating lots of little knights. If you haven't guessed it, that is an accurate description of myself as the scary giant! Try and describe yourself as a scary creature, even if you are a pretty little king or queen. Let the knights know that you are a sleepy giant, but you are a light sleeper, so if you hear any noise you will wake up and grind their bones to make your bread. If the players aren't old enough to understand this is a game, just say you will come and get them. Knights are safe once they are outside of the circle at the far end from the cave. Make the cave out of soccer goals and put all of the balls in there. Each knight must rescue their soccer ball princesses and princes and get them back to the safe area. Move to the middle of the circle and start to fall asleep with a yawn and a stumble before hitting the deck with a bang. I generally wake up straight away and remind players to tip toe past the giant, not to run and giggle. This will not work completely, but it's the thought that counts. Wake up two or three times more and chase the brave knights away from the cave, stopping some of the knights in their tracks and putting their princesses and princes back to the cave before sleeping again. Do not let a player take someone else's ball as we want every player to get a little success, regardless of how shy. This takes a little longer, and you can ask other knights to help the new soccer players if you wish, but stay asleep until they eventually accomplish the task.

Once everyone has rescued their soccer balls, use the movement technique before bringing the knights all together and review the session. Make sure the technique of shooting is reviewed and the technique is described once more before sending them away.

Bring the coaches in and discuss how the last games went in regards to skill development. Hopefully you will have some positive responses with players who performed well in the new skill environment, but remember, Rome wasn't built in a day. Give it time and keep supporting the coaches. Now we are working on a technique rather than individual skill, explain how the two are somewhat conflicting. Skill is primarily keeping the ball, whereas with the technique aspect of shooting we are asking the players to kick the ball away. Both can still be performed if we allow players to first do a skill before they can shoot. If we add shooting, we are progressing the skill to the final level, to add a final product. Keep the focus on the skill and technique of shooting, nothing more. It is extremely tempting to try and correct everything we see that goes wrong, but refrain so as not overload the young minds.

SESSION TOPIC	KEY COACHING POINTS
Knights of the Round Table (Shooting)	1. The standing foot is level with the ball and pointing at the target 2. Use the laces of the cleat with the toe pointed down 3. Point the leg of the kicking foot to the target after impact

Session Story: Our soccer players have become knights of the round table. Every part of the session is inside a circle of cones. Our knights have a coat of armour (pinnies) and they travel, learning the trade of a knight as they fight past witches, fight for princesses and princes and sneak past giants on their adventure

ARCHERS AT THE READY

Set up a cone in the middle of a large circle with enough cones spaced around it for all players. Each player gets a ball and stands by a cone. The cone in the middle has a ball balanced on top of it. On the coach's call, everyone shoots and tries to knock the ball off. Have the players run and retrieve a ball and set up to play again.

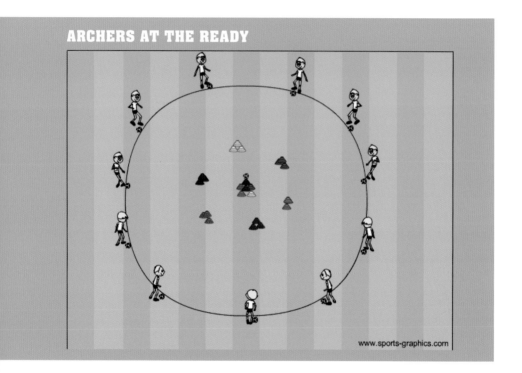

ARCHERS AT THE READY

www.sports-graphics.com

Coaching points: 1. Stand level with the ball and point at the target

2. Use the laces of the cleat with the toe pointed down

3. Point the leg of the kicking foot to the target after impact

GRAB THE WICKED WITCH

(Freeze Tag) All players start on one side of the field with a ball. Coach turns his or her back to the players, and they can move forward. The coach then turns back around and the players need to freeze with their foot on the ball. All players should have moved forward and now stand still with one foot on the ball. Any player still moving or without his or her ball gets sent back to the starting line.

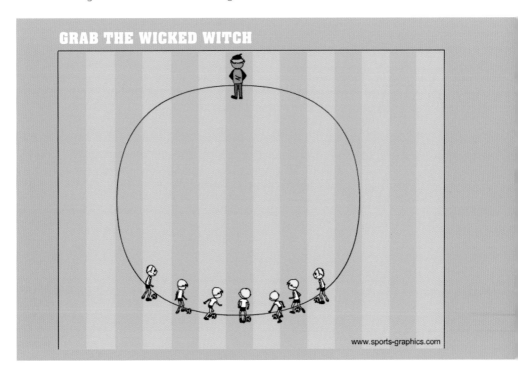

GRAB THE WICKED WITCH

www.sports-graphics.com

Coaching points: 1. Push the ball along slowly

2. Use the laces of the cleat with the toe pointed down to move the ball

3. Keep in contact with the ball

BATTLE FOR THE MAIDEN

The ball has magically transformed into a sword. The players move around in the circle and attempt to hit their swords against each other's. The kids make noise whenever the swords collide. If a player gets hit by a sword, they can come over to the wizard (the coach) who can heal them and send them back into the game. Towards the end, the wizard turns into the black knight and all the players try to chop the wizard down with their swords by kicking their balls at the coach.

BATTLE FOR THE MAIDEN

www.sports-graphics.com

Coaching points: 1. Stand level with the ball and point at the target

2. Use the laces of the cleat with the toe pointed down

3. Point the leg of the kicking foot to the target after impact

SLEEPING GIANT

The coach sleeps in a goal at one end with all the soccer balls a few feet away on the field. The players start in the goal at the opposite end. The players have to quietly creep up to the soccer balls and steal them from the giant without waking him and shoot the balls back into their base. If the giant wakes he can chase the kids and get whatever soccer balls that aren't in the base back and fall back asleep again.

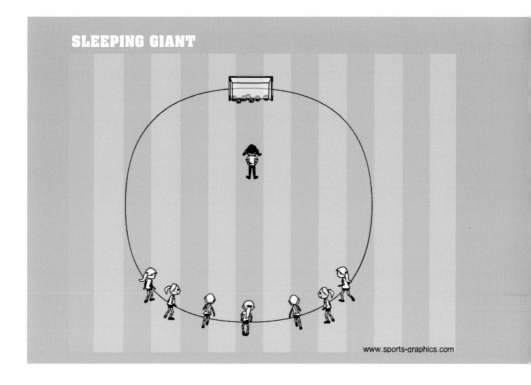

SLEEPING GIANT

www.sports-graphics.com

Coaching points: 1. Stand level with the ball and point at the target

2. Use the laces of the cleat with the toe pointed down

3. Point the leg of the kicking foot to the target after impact

E. DRIVING SCHOOL

Today we will be teaching our little soccer players how to drive, and as this is a serious matter, discipline is of the utmost importance. You are the educator and assessor of the laws on the road, the Driving Instructor. In the past, players are allowed to dribble the ball freely, but not today as every collision is dangerous for our learner drivers.

Use the movement technique and take them to a corner, going over the ground rules (bad hands, good feet and naughty toes) before allowing them to guess about what today's adventure may be. Tell them how you are the driving instructor who is going to teach them how to drive their very own soccer ball car. Explain to them early how important it is to not crash their car or bodies during the whole session. This should get the learner drivers to constantly look around and keep their heads up throughout the session.

Now it is time to go to the showroom and pick their cars. Take the players to another corner and keep them on their feet as they pick the cars they are to use. Get the young drivers to put their keys in the ignition and make the sounds of their cars. Remind the drivers that they must not bump into anyone or hit their car soccer ball against another car. If they do, they have to go to the mechanic and talk about the damage. The mechanic will be you if no other coaches are at hand. If you have an assistant, this is a great chance for them to express the importance of going slower and being more in control of the soccer ball when dribbling.

Part 1: The first part of the session is Driver's Ed. Before we are allowed to drive on the streets, we must understand and obey the rules of the road. Our little learner drivers are to dribble around and show control as they keep their heads up and avoid hitting other learner drivers. Make sure the players understand how to stop the ball instantly by putting their foot on the ball and making the sound of the breaks screeching. Once they are doing well, instruct the learner drivers how to make basic turns. Tell the learner drivers to drive to a side of the square. Once there, they are to initially stop, look all around them and turn either left or right depending on the space. If there is lots of space in one direction, turn that way with an inside cut. Show the technique to the players and then set them loose on the road as you coach their turns and decision-making abilities. Once they are doing well with this, teach the outside cut turn and reversing (with either side to sides or toe taps), ensuring the process is repeated so learner drivers are focusing on one skill at a time. For advanced drivers you may also teach the emergency turn and windshield wipers in this environment. After focusing on one skill at a time, allow the learner drivers to express themselves and select whatever skill they wish to use at the boundary. Once they have gained a level of success, send the drivers to go put gas in their car (otherwise known as a water break).

Part 2: Now is the time for our learner drivers to gain respect for the law. Ask the players to line up beside each other on one side of the square. You are the policeman ready to lay down the law to any learner drivers who are driving irresponsibly. The learner drivers must travel from one side of town to the other without having their ball

impounded by the police. If they are in control of their ball and they stay away from the police, then they are allowed to travel freely, but if the slightest lack of control is seen, the police will kick their soccer ball cars to the pound on either side of the square. As a policeman who believes in rehabilitation, we will give the learner drivers an opportunity to make up for their reckless driving and make them police cadets. Unfortunately for the law abiding citizens, the new cadets are a little wild, and they are after arrests. The learner drivers will have to drive a little faster and keep the ball close if they are to make it to the other side of town. Keep on playing until the last driver remains. Get the learner drivers to honk their horns if they are ready and for the police to sound their sirens prior to every trip across town. Remember, the louder they are, the more fun they and you will have. Feel free to play the game more than once if you have the time before sending the players for a water break.

Part 3: Now our law abiding citizens are finished topping off their tanks, it's time to go on the road for real. The pressure is on to keep their cars under control as they drive around town, but before we go anywhere, the learner drivers need to understand basic rules of the road. Get the players together with the movement technique and tell them about this stag of the adventure. We as instructors are watching to make sure they are driving correctly, but first, every learner driver needs to know the basic colors. Ask them what the red light means. They should say "stop," so show them how we stop the car by putting our foot on the ball and making the breaks screech as we did in part 1 of the session. Ask the learner drivers what the green light means. They should say "go," and then ask what the yellow light means. They should say "slow." Now set them off on the road and give them the different color commands. Once they have a good grasp on the game, it is time to push the drivers to their limits. As the professional driving instructor, you know many maneuvers you can perform with the automobiles. There are many suggestions in the skill breakdown section of the book. Feel free to select skills from there, such as windshield wipers, U-turn, and all the different color lights, or make some up yourself for what you want the learner drivers to learn.

This is a great method to introduce new skills or build on some of the skills you currently use. Start by showing a skill at red light, then asking them to do the skill under yellow light before moving the players on by requesting the skill on green light. This will help

each player add pace to the technique, which will enable the player to gain confidence prior to using the move against someone. Feel free to progress the game even further by changing the commands from verbal to visual. Different color pinnies, cones, or even holding up a set number of fingers can relate to a skill the players need to do. Now all of our players are skill freaks (I mean professional race car drivers), it's time to take a little pit stop and relax before the all-important driving exam.

Part 4: Ok, instructor, it is time to see if all your hard work and dedication has paid off. Have your learner drivers learned enough to get them through their driving test? Will they crack under the pressure? Will they pick their nose? It is time to find out. Reduce

your playing area significantly. The size of your square should be just big enough to allow every learner driver to stand side by side on two sides of the square. Explain how the test will operate by describing the stage of the exam and then performing the stage prior to moving on. If a driver's car crashes into another, they fail the exam. The stages are as follows:

1. **Cross the grid:** Each learner driver must make it from one side to the other directly opposite. Each side will cross alone while the other group waits for each learner driver to finish before the second side is allowed to start.

2. **Cross the grid together:** Each learner driver must make it from one side to the other directly opposite all at the same time. The crossing of learner drivers will make the task twice as difficult, ensuring all drivers are completely focused.

3. **Cross the grid twice:** Each learner drivers must make it from one side to the other directly opposite and back again, all at the same time. If a 180-degree turn was taught during your session, use this to turn back. Otherwise you may wish to reverse backward or perform two cuts to turn around at the halfway point. Feel free to give learner drivers a helpful tip about looking behind them before they turn.

Most of the time all learner drivers make it unscathed, but on occasion a learner driver may crash. I would certainly use your discretion, driving instructor, on whether the driver should pass or fail, but make sure you deal with these individuals last after the session is over. For now, take everyone to the DMV to get their license. Use the movement technique and once in a corner, take a picture of each driver and hand them their driving license. Once every learner driver has their license in hand, finish the session and kindly remind them they can only drive a soccer ball. The last thing you need is a 7-year-old jumping into the driver's seat of the minivan thinking they can really drive now! Any learner driver who has failed, let them know the importance of keeping their car close and under control before awarding them with their driving license. These players are too young to understand the "tough love" treatment from a non-parent and remember, you never know what might be happening at home (unless this is your child, then feel free to do whatever you like).

For our coaches discussion today, use a little psychology to get your results. Understanding each coach takes pride in what they are doing for their kids, we cannot dictate what we want directly all the time as coaches will get upset if we tell them they can do better. Instead, isolate a few coaches who are doing well and specific instances of success. Tell the group of instances during the game and practices where you are impressed with a few coaches. They may have taken a player to the side and coached them 1-on-1 to describe the skill and technique effectively. A coach may have had an effective conversation with the parents prior to the game and told them what we are looking for from the players. Someone could have created a scoring system for their team on who can do the most skills. A coach can be effective on coaching the skill during the game. Tell the coaches of these instances and inspire others to want praise. This is no different from the players. If you tell someone to do anything, there is a lack of desire involved and on some instances you will receive a push back from them. However, if you make it public how proud you are of a specific player for performing what you want, others will try harder to get the praise. They will come to you and ask for your help more frequently, which will sometimes happen with the coaches. Now expect the coaches to ask you and each other for advice on how to be more effective.

SESSION TOPIC	KEY COACHING POINTS
Driving School (90- and 180-degree turns)	1. Use the correct technique 2. Fast feet 3. Accelerate away

Session Story: Today is the first day the kids will get to drive their very own car. In the dealership they get to pick their cars and show you what noise they make. Their magical keys can start their soccer ball engines and from there, they will learn how to drive as they learn how to turn, stop, dodge traffic, and even get away from the police.

DRIVER'S ED

Each player selects a car at the car park and starts their car by putting the key in the ignition and making car noises (the ball is the car). Have the players drive within a square area (the more players, the larger the area). Increase and decrease speed as they progress. When anyone reaches a boundary, instruct them to make either a reverse or left or right turn. Have all players avoid crashing and have them race to return the car to the designated parking area at the end. Add as many turns as you wish within this environment.

DRIVER'S ED

www.sports-graphics.com

Coaching points: 1. Use the correct technique

2. Fast feet

3. Accelerate away

DODGE THE POLICEMAN

All the players except one are behind one end line and attempt to make it to the other end line past the policeman. The player who is the policeman has to arrest as many players as he or she can before they are in their safe zone. The policeman must gain full possession of the ball for it to count. When a player has their ball stolen, they become policemen. Last player with a ball wins.

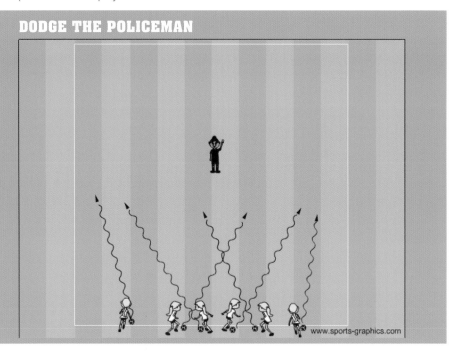

DODGE THE POLICEMAN

www.sports-graphics.com

Coaching points: 1. Use the correct technique

2. Fast feet

3. Accelerate away

RED LIGHT, GREEN LIGHT

This is a great game for introducing new skills. The kids dribble around when the coach says, "green light." When the coach says, "red light," the players stop with their foot on the ball. New colors are added and with every color the player must perform a certain maneuver of the coach's choice.

Coaching points: 1. Use the correct technique

2. Fast feet

3. Accelerate away

RUSH HOUR TRAFFIC

Create a square playing area roughly 10 feet by 10 feet. Divide the players into two groups. Set one group up on the north side of the square and the other team on the east side. Each player has a ball. On the start all players must cross the square, make the turn when they get to the other side, and come back. Use the 180-degree turn you taught earlier in the session and make it a race to see which team can be the first to get its players across and back three times.

RUSH HOUR TRAFFIC

www.sports-graphics.com

Coaching points: 1. Use the correct technique

2. Fast feet

3. Accelerate away

F.   FUNKY CHICKEN ISLAND ADVENTURE

This session is by far my favorite for allowing players to have fun with soccer as you, the coach, lower all inhibitions and have fun with future soccer legends. Today, our fearless exploration leader, we are going on an adventure, an expedition to find the most elusive of all creatures: The Funky Chicken. As we are on an expedition, feel free to get into character as an old time Lewis and Clark/Marco Polo/Charles Darwin–like figure with the khaki shorts and hat, or go the Dora the Explorer–route. To complete a passing and receiving session with young explorers is a feat in itself, so the character we portray and environment we create will determine the success of the session.

Begin with the movement technique and get the tempo nice and high for the story about the hunt for the funky chicken. Take our young explorers to a corner where they are not looking into the sun and go over the ground rules before explaining our adventure. Make sure every explorer is well versed in the bad hands, good feet and naughty toes rules before asking who wants to go on an adventure. Listen to all the weird and wacky suggestions before telling the explorers what we are going to do today: We are traveling to Funky Chicken Island on the hunt for the funky chicken. The funky chicken is huge with a big beak, long legs, and lots and lots of pretty, colorful feathers that are worth millions and billions and bajillions of dollars!! (Yes, I am aware that bajillions is not an actual amount, but you get the point.) Also, the funky chicken lays giant golden eggs which are also worth millions and billions and bajillions of dollars! But getting to the funky chicken is not easy, and we are going to have to work together as a team to work our way through Funky Chicken Island and capture the funky chicken. Can you help? (Get the explorers to shout louder and louder with every answer as you build the excitement. Do this by asking the questions louder and louder.) Are we going to work together? Are you ready to find the funky chicken? LET'S GO! With that, get up and get moving around your playing area, asking the explorers to follow.

Part 1: Prior to the first game, I generally think of all the ways we can travel to the island. Dribble around and ask the explorers how we could get there. Allow the explorers to make suggestions and be creative on how you would dribble your ball around to replicate their suggestions. If an explorer suggests flying, for instance, we can make everyone use a helicopter and run around with their arms out, turning in circles with the ball as they fly around. By accident, explorers will use the inside or outside cut circles skill. Guide their suggestions slightly to get all modes of transport you wish to use, such as airplane, ship, swimming, canoe, submarine, speedboat, etc. Arrive at the island and take all explorers to one corner of the square. Let the players know of the hazardous beach ahead of them, which is controlled by the scary sand monsters. Demonstrate when a sand monster tags someone how they lift their soccer ball high in the air with their bad hands, open their legs really wide, and shout, "Help, help, I'm stuck in the sand!" Show how an explorer becomes unfrozen by passing the ball through their legs with the insides of their feet. This is a difficult task for young children because many could not tell you where the insides of their feet are in the first place. Here is how I help the kids locate this surface: Get them all to put their hands together in front of them, and turn the hands around so your palms are pointing outward. Now put your hands between your feet and pat the part of your foot next to your hands. Select one sand monster for every eight explorers and send them out to tag the players. Leaders of the exploration can be sand monsters, but understand that if all coaches are chasing players, there is no one to coach the passing technique. If all explorers become stuck in the sand or the sand monsters become tired, select new sand monsters and start over.

Part 2: Now we are through the treacherous beach, it is time to explore a little farther. As in every adventure filled with mystery and danger, we arrive at the rickety old bridge. As you can imagine, the bridge is made of rotten old wood and rope that looks perilously close to breaking at any moment. If we are to get all our equipment across before it breaks, we must be quick and work together as a team. Use this story to give the explorers an idea of the tempo and alertness needed for this part of the session to work. Any passing and receiving element is extremely tough at this age, and for the most part should be rarely worked on, but it is important for the explorers to know the technique of passing. Once the story has been told, move the explorers to one sideline and separate them into teams. The explorers will be spread out across the width of the square, approximately 4 yards apart, so get an idea of how many explorers should be in a line with regards to the size of your playing area. I suggest around five to six players in each team. Make sure there is an explorer with all the balls on one side of the bridge

(or playing area), one explorer on the other side of the bridge directly opposite without balls, and explorers spread out evenly between. Once the teams are in position, it is a race to see who can get their exploring equipment (soccer balls) to the other side. This is a great chance to make sure every explorer is using the inside of their foot to receive, turn, and look at their teammate who they are to pass to, and then pass using the inside of their foot. Once we have gone across the bridge once, add the next coaching point of pointing the standing foot toward the target for accuracy and play once more. If a team is dominating, feel free to add a few balls to the winning team's equipment pile at the beginning of the bridge when they are not looking.

Part 3: Save the Funky Chicken Egg can be played in two different ways. The diagram and information on the session plan is for the U8 players with good coordination. If you do not have these players on your team, look at the following second description.

Now we are safely across the bridge, let us continue the hunt. Take our explorers on a hunt using the movement technique before arriving back at the same place where we finished the rickety old bridge part of the session. Keep the explorers in the same teams and put all the team's balls back on the cone once more. If you have a younger group, I suggest coming straight back from the water break to the balls because it sometimes proves difficult to reorganize the explorers. Once there we explain how we are at the funky chicken's nest. The funky chicken lays heavy, fragile golden eggs, which are worth millions and billions and bajillions of dollars! But how are we going to get them back to the boat? The eggs are so heavy that when we hold one, we cannot move our feet. Also, we do not want to throw them because they are way too heavy to throw, plus they may break and the team will have to go back to the start again. So how can we move the eggs from one side to the other? Allow the players to explore their minds and make suggestions, with a little guidance from you, until they make a chain and move the ball along, like pass the parcel, with their hands from one explorer to the other. When the ball gets to the last explorer in the chain, we will see how we are not at the boat yet, so what do we do now? Guide their answers once more to move off of the ball and get to the end of the chain. This part of the session is to develop movement off the ball, so constantly say "pass and move" or "give and go," so explorers realize as soon as they pass, they must move to support the play. Again, create a race between the teams, and let's play! Enforce the rules and constantly encourage development because the race element will create the tempo we wish. After the game has finished, with the teams all winning, send them away for a water break and get ready for the most fun you will ever have as an adult (potentially).

Part 4: Get a bag of pinnies and get the players moving. Take them to a corner and ask them to lay on their tummies with the ball by their side and hands over their eyes. Make sure all heads are down on the ground and let the explorers know that if anyone looks up, you will stop telling the story, and we will not see the funky chicken.

Now, move behind all the explorers and begin the story. As you tell the story of the funky chicken, stuff as many pinnies as you can all over your body, except areas where the pinnies may hang over your private parts. You do not want a child grabbing what they shouldn't for reasons I hope we all understand. Tuck them in your cleats, socks, jersey, shorts, neck, around the wrists, head, and hold some in your hands so you become completely covered. As you do this the story you tell goes a little something like this:

Years and years ago on a small island in the middle of the ocean lived a mad scientist. He wanted to become rich, so he came up with an idea: to create a funky chicken. He went out onto the island and found a chicken. He took the chicken home and put him on the operating table. He attached electrodes all over the chicken and turned his funky chicken machine on. The lights flickered and the building began to shake until it all went dark and quiet. The scientist turned on the light, and a beautiful, colorful funky chicken with magical feathers was standing on the table. Now the mad scientist made a big mistake, he forgot to close the window, and the funky chicken ran out of the building and away somewhere on the island. The mad scientist hunted for years and years, and when the mad scientist saw the funky chicken, he could not catch him. The funky chicken was too fast. But I have some good news: Before we came to the island I met a guy who told me that if you have your soccer ball at your feet, the funky chicken slows down, maybe just slow enough for you to reach out and pluck a magical feather from the funky chicken. Beware, if you do not have your ball close to you, the funky chicken will be too fast for you to catch.

With this, run away and hide behind some of the spectators. Wait for the explorers to get up and look around, which may take some time. If you have another coach out there, ask them to wake the explorers after you have hidden. If not, be patient, they will come eventually. Let the kids search around until you are spotted and they get a little closer, then go crazy! Run around making chicken noises. The crazier you are at this moment, the better it is for everyone. I am not an acrobat, but I do throw in the occasional forward roll or cartwheel away from the kids so I do not inadvertently kick someone in the face. Run toward the explorers who are keeping their ball close to them and subsequently run away from those who are moving without their ball. Once all the magical feathers are plucked, lie down and take a well earned breath or two. If you

have done this correctly, you should be a little exhausted. Congratulate the explorers on their success and ask on the count of three to throw the feathers in the air so we can all share in the magic. Get the explorers to leave the pinnies and take them to a corner to evaluate the session and the techniques taught. Ask explorers if they can remember how to pass and what they must remember to do every time. Also ask about what the players need to do once they pass the ball to a teammate before sending the explorers on their way.

By now we should have a good level of buy in to the program from your coaches. For us to be truly effective, we need to add the final level of influence to our program: the parents. If the coaches have the parental support, they will feel more confident to try more with the players. Ask the coach to hold a little team meeting prior to the game or at a training session if all parents or parental units are in attendance. This can happen earlier in the season, bit only do so if you have full support from the coaches already. Remember, we did this after the first session to take the pressure off the coaches, so asking our coaches to do this from the beginning may be a little too much for them to handle all at once. Think of other ways to communicate with the parents such as email and social media. The coaches will always be grateful for the support.

SESSION TOPIC	KEY COACHING POINTS
Funky Chicken Island (Passing)	1. The standing foot is level with the ball and pointing at the target 2. Use the inside of the foot to pass the ball 3. Present the inside of the kicking foot to the targret

Session Story: The players arrive on Funky Chicken Island looking for the funky chicken. The journey to find him is a hard fought encounter because they have to fight through quicksand and cross old bridges for their mission to save a funky chicken egg and to take the funky chicken's magical feathers!

STUCK IN THE SAND

Set up an in-bounds area and give each player a ball except for one. The player without the ball is "it" and tries to freeze you by touching (not kicking) your ball. When this happens the player is frozen and must lift the ball above his or her head and spread the legs wide to create a "goal." The player can be unfrozen when another player kicks the ball through the frozen players legs. Play until all players are frozen or the player that is "it" is exhausted.

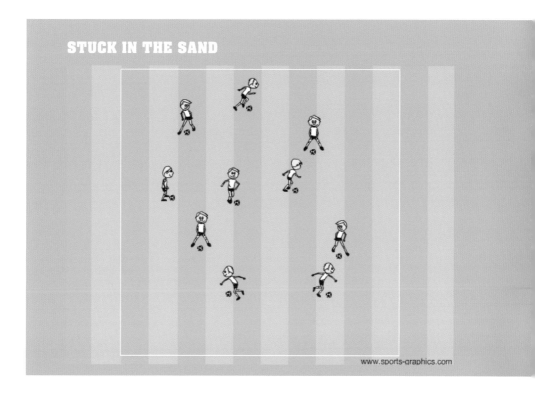

STUCK IN THE SAND

www.sports-graphics.com

Coaching points:
1. The standing foot is level with the ball and pointing at the target
2. Use the inside of the foot to pass the ball
3. Present the inside of the kicking foot to the target

CROSS THE RICKETY OLD BRIDGE

Depending on the number of players, divide them into two or three equal groups. Line the players up in evenly spaced parallel lines. Vary the distance between players based on skill and type of pass you have them execute. Start with simple instep passes. The first player in line passes to the next who must trap the ball and make the turn to pass to the next player. Begin with the players making their own choice in which foot to use and then increase the complexity. Have them trap left, pass right, or trap right and pass left. There is no end to the different ways to do this game:

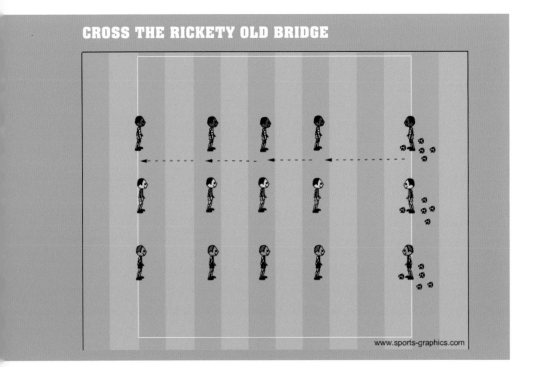

CROSS THE RICKETY OLD BRIDGE

www.sports-graphics.com

Coaching points: 1. The standing foot is level with the ball and pointing at the target
2. Use the inside of the foot to pass the ball
3. Present the inside of the kicking foot to the target

SAVE THE FUNKY CHICKEN EGG

It is played like Ultimate Frisbee. Divide the players into two equal teams and have them set up on either end of the field. Establish an end zone at each end with cones. One team will start with the ball in their hands. The player with the ball cannot move, but he or she can pivot on one foot like in basketball. If the ball hits the ground, the opposing team gains possession. The team will pass to a teammate to move the ball up the field. The goal is to move the ball up the field to a player in the end zone area who scores by catching the ball in the end zone. The team without control of the ball should try to intercept passes and mark open players, but the defensive players cannot steal the ball directly from a player's hands.

SAVE THE FUNKY CHICKEN EGG

www.sports-graphics.com

Coaching points: 1. Quick ball movement

2. Movement of the ball

3. Vision

THE HUNT FOR THE FUNKY CHICKEN

The coach asks the players to lie on the ground face down and their hands over their eyes for story time. The coach then tells the story of the funky chicken. The coach then makes up a story of the funky chicken and why he is on the island. The chicken has magical feathers which are worth a million dollars, and it is our chance to be millionaires! The great news is someone told you the secret of getting one of the magical feathers from the chicken. The only way is to have a soccer ball at your feet. As you tell the story, place pinnies in your socks, t-shirt, shorts, cleats, wherever you can. At the end of the story, go hide behind one of the parents and wait for the kids to come find you. Once you are spotted, go crazy! Jump around and make chicken noises, do cartwheels, and roll around until all the feathers are gone.

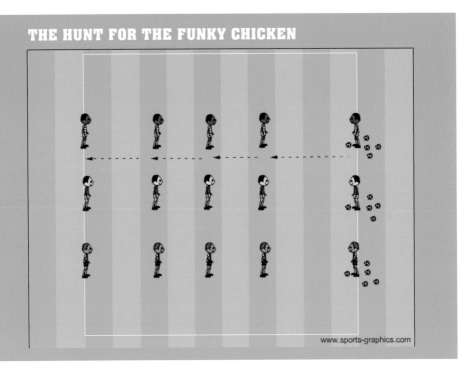

THE HUNT FOR THE FUNKY CHICKEN

www.sports-graphics.com

Coaching points: 1. Have fun!

2. Have fun!

3. Have fun!

G.   ALIEN INVASION

Well, coaches, the unexpected has happened, aliens do exist and they are coming to take over the planet. As in the case of many heroes, fate chooses them, and today, fate has chosen you to command our soccer players to safety. Be strong, commander; you must guide our rebel alliance of star troopers to protect our planet before leading the attack against the aliens.

We start the session normally by using the movement technique to get the star troopers moving and the heart rates up. Take them to a corner and go over the ground rules once more. By now the players should be well versed with quick and loud responses. Still allow their imaginations to go wild as they give you suggestions on what adventure they want to go on before setting the scene.

Part 1: Tell the players to look up, far beyond the sky. Tell them that in outer space there are aliens who are trying to take over our planet. Ask the star troopers about all the things they love about planet Earth, things like mommy, daddy, pets, chocolate, etc. Now let the star troopers know that their soccer ball is their planet that they must protect from the evil, ugly aliens and their lasers. If a laser hits the soccer ball planet, then their planet will explode. Point out who the aliens are and explain the boundary before the big count down: 3.......2......1.....the aliens are here! Take a hand full of cones and throw them at the soccer balls. Make random alien noises (use your imagination on this one) and make large explosions when you hit a planet soccer ball. Once the aliens run out of lasers, stop the star troopers and explain how to shield the ball from the evil alien lasers. This is a tactical element of skill development. We are teaching the players to keep their bodies between the ball and the defender, so get a player to demonstrate this. Hopefully someone has been doing this pretty well during the initial alien attack, but if not, select anyone who can help. Ask them to stand directly between the ball and the alien, and then throw a few lasers at their legs. Get frustrated as the lasers bounce off the legs harmlessly, leaving the star troopers safe and sound. Now move around and ask the star trooper to move, keeping between the ball and the alien. Lastly, ask the star trooper to turn and face the ball as they keep their butt toward the defender. This should be more than enough for most players, but for the elite-level players, ask them to move the ball with their ball mastery skills as well. Now when we attack the planets, assist anyone who needs help in their shielding technique instead of an all out offensive on their planets. Once all the lasers are gone, ask the star troopers who has protected their planet from the evil aliens? Celebrate by running around, jumping and screaming for joy with hands in the air before sending them away for a quick water break.

Part 2: With our last week's topic being passing, we are going to touch on this once more with this part of the session. We are to take the fight to the aliens and fly into outer space. As with all alien ships, the vessel is protected by a large force field, which we need to break. As the star troopers are on their water break, ask the other commanders for help in making lots of 2-yard gates around the playing area. These gates are the alien force field where the star troopers need to pass a ball through to weaken and eventually break the alien defenses. The hardest part of the session is the organization

commander, so get the star troopers back and use the movement technique before taking them outside of your playing area. Ask the star troopers to find a partner and for them to hold hands. I know this is a little weird for older players and adults to do, but at this age players should hold hands without too much fuss. Ask them to choose one ball to use and to follow you. Groups will still have two balls, but with moving them, you will see which pair has listened and understood your instructions and which has not. Remove one ball from those groups and make sure everyone is ready to play. Demonstrate what the star troopers need to do by using another commander or a star trooper for your partner. Take them to a gate and pass the ball through. Once the ball goes through the gate, get both players to make a large explosion noise and raise their hands in the air to show they have weakened the force field. Move to another gate and show how we are to move off the ball and communicate. Also, make sure you explain the passing technique to the players so they remember the key points of what we are looking for (use the inside of the foot, standing foot pointed to the target, and follow through, showing the inside of your foot to your partner). Send them away in their pairs and once everyone has a strong grip on what we are looking to do, set a number of explosions we need before the force field will explode. Count every explosion you see until we hit the target number and celebrate once more in a similar fashion as before.

Part 3: You have done well up to now, commander, but now is when you are really tested. We are about to board the alien mother ship. Use the movement technique before telling the star troopers how we need to get to the bridge where the queen and king alien is commanding their fleet and take them down. Explain how many years ago, you were beamed up into space by aliens. They did all kinds of experiments on you, but you managed to get away. Because of this, you know your way around the alien mother ship and all of the secret passages to avoid the millions of aliens on board. If they listen and follow you, we can take down the aliens once and for all. Ask the star troopers if they are ready in a whisper, and they should whisper back. This technique will get the star troopers ready to be quiet and not disturb any of the aliens. Tip toe away, touching the soccer ball every time you lift your feet, ask the star troopers to follow you, using the same technique. Your other commanders, if you have any, should be there to guide the players behind you with all the skills we are about to introduce. Look at chapter

6 for skill suggestions and how to do each skill as you open doors, climb up ladders, and the windy ramp and how to be invisible before finding the ammunitions locker and shooting lasers. Do this for a good amount of time because this is the topic of today's session. Once all of the star troopers become proficient at the skills, take them to the door of the bridge and send them away for a quick water break.

Part 4: Once our star troopers are back, remind them of how to use their lasers. If you do not, star troopers will zing balls at you straight away instead of using the laser technique. Now get everyone to open the door with their soccer balls and introduce them to the ugliest, scariest, largest aliens they have ever seen. That would be you. Tell the star troopers to attack the aliens using their lasers. You may wish to precede this by a demonstration of what will happen if they shoot their lasers at an alien. Ask the aliens to make a funny, crazy noise if they get hit by a laser and demonstrate this in

front of the kids. This should get the star troopers giggling away and hopefully keen to shoot lasers rather than pinging the balls at you. Do this for several minutes until the lasers run out of power, so all that is left is for the star troopers to throw (kick) their lasers at the aliens and hope for the best. Now the star troopers are allowed to kick the soccer balls at you, do your best to die dramatically as the academy award actor that you are, before celebrating with the star troopers and taking them to a corner to evaluate the session.

In the evaluation, go over the skills they have used to get around the alien mother ship and quiz the star troopers on how they could use them during a game. Ask them if they can shield the ball from a defender using any of the skills, including skills that do not work. For instance, can you shield the ball climbing the ladder? Hopefully the star troopers see that toe taps are not efficient in keeping the ball away from a defender. Then ask if climbing the windy ramp is good for shielding the ball from a defender? If anyone disagrees, use them for a demonstration and see if he or she can get the ball from you as you turn with the ball, keeping your body between them and the ball. Challenge the star troopers to see if anyone can do this during the game on the weekend before sending them back to planet earth and to their parents.

It's time to inspire our coaches once more, so let us start by finding out their progress from the parent meeting. Some will have forgotten to do this, but take joy from those who did. You will get a lot of parents wanting this approach for the kids, with a rare parent wanting their child to care about winning. Help this coach to handle such parents and support them if they need you to speak to the specific parent. We have just finished a skills-based session, so challenge the coaches to see who can get their team to do the most skills this weekend? Perhaps provide a reward to the winner and speak to them on how they can record the skills. Ask an assistant coach, a parent, or someone from the organization to record this. Now the coaches are challenged, reluctant coaches who are still on a mission to win will have a new challenge for everlasting victory and pride.

SESSION TOPIC	KEY COACHING POINTS
Alien Invasion (Ball mastery)	1. Use the correct technique 2. Fast feet 3. Head and eyes up

Session Story: Oh no, aliens are trying to invade the planet! But not to worry, our fearless soccer players are here to protect the planet and to take down the alien invasion with their amazing ball mastery skills

PROTECT THE PLANET

Each player has a planet to protect from the alien (the coach). The alien is trying to blow up the world by shooting flying saucers at their planets. The flying saucers are cones which the coach is trying to Frisbee toward the soccer balls. The players can dribble away in the area and use their bodies to protect their planets. A planet needs to be hit three times for it to explode, but the coach never hits a planet more than twice so everyone stays involved.

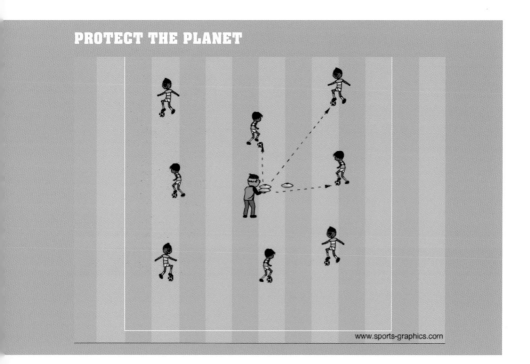

PROTECT THE PLANET

www.sports-graphics.com

Coaching points: 1. Keep your body between the coach and the ball

2. Keep your head up to be aware of where the coach is

3. Move into the space away from the coach

BREAK THE ALIEN MOTHER SHIP'S FORCE FIELD

Have each player get a partner and a ball between the two. The teams spread out on the sideline. Set up the field by placing sets of cones about 2 to 4 feet apart (to create a gate) all over the playing area. When the coach says "go," one player dribbles the ball out and makes a pass through any gate to their teammate. The teammate then dribbles the ball to the next goal to make the pass through. The players can go through the gates in any order they want, but they must pass to their teammate through every set of cones before returning to the sideline with their ball. Every pass weakens the force field, and when all teams have finished, the force field is broken. To add ball mastery, every time a player receives the ball they have to perform a skill before moving on.

www.sports-graphics.com

Coaching points: 1. Use the correct technique

2. Fast feet

3. Head and eyes up

TAKING DOWN THE MOTHER SHIP

The players dribble around when the coach creates an order, such as invisibility: the players have to perform balance circles and they become invisible. Create multiple commands and visual cues for players to perform certain maneuvers, such as holding a cone in the air could be an alien which we need to do toe taps to get away. Use colored pinnies and key words to get as many skills out as you wish.

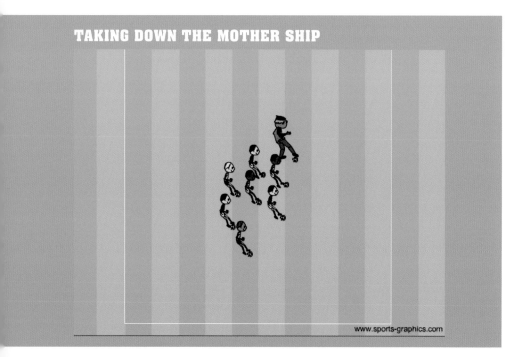

TAKING DOWN THE MOTHER SHIP

www.sports-graphics.com

Coaching points: 1. Use the correct technique

2. Fast feet

3. Head and eyes up

ATTACK THE ALIEN

Each player has a ball. Pick an inbounds area and use cones to establish it. The younger the children, the smaller the playing area should be. On the coach's call, the game starts. The players dribble the ball around and try to hit the coach, who is running all around in the inbounds area as the alien king or squeen. After they hit the coach, the coach has to make an alien noise. Keep going until the alien cannot take any more and the players win!

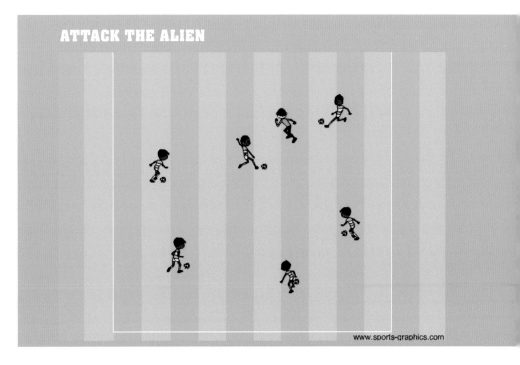

ATTACK THE ALIEN

www.sports-graphics.com

Coaching points: 1. Have fun!

2. Have fun!

3. Have fun!

H.   UNDER THE SEA ADVENTURE

Today we are leading the young scuba divers through the ocean on the Under the Sea Adventure. You will be their scuba instructor as we look for sunken treasure, the remains of pirate ships from years past, full of gold and jewels. But beware: The deadly creatures of the sea stand in our way, so we must be prepared to use our evasive techniques if we are to take all the treasure home. Describe the adventure to the players after all the usual formalities before describing the first part of the session.

Part 1: Luckily for us, today we have a helpful guide fish (our soccer ball) that has lived in the ocean for years and will take us to the sunken pirate ship full of treasure. However, the fish is a little excitable and can get away from us at times. We are going to learn how to keep the fish under control by stopping it with many different parts of our bodies. Beware, the fish is a little slippery, and we will have to work hard if we are to stop the fish. Get the scuba kids to stop their fish by calling out a body part. Once all have stopped their fish, tell them to dribble away. Keep doing this, using multiple parts of their bodies. Feel free to name multiple body parts, one after the other, to get the scuba kids moving fast. Now their heart rates and excitement are up, we can teach them the defenses of the sea. As their scuba instructor, you are aware of how to defend yourself against these terrible creatures, so instruct them on the maneuvers they need to protect themselves from specific sea creatures. Refer to chapter 6 on the specific techniques to teach and how to perform the skills. I would suggest focusing on no more than three skills to make sure they can remember what you teach them. Overloading the players with too many skills at once can have an adverse effect on development. Better to be perfect at a few skills than average at many. Once you are happy with their techniques, instructor, you are ready to follow our fishes to the deep blue ocean in hunt for treasure. Send the scuba kids away for refueling before the big adventure.

Part 2: I hope you are a masterful instructor and our little scuba kids are ready to brave the deep ocean, fraught with danger. Especially as the scuba kids are in competition with each other on who will make it to the sunken treasure. Pair the kids up with one ball between two, as we did in the Alien Invasion adventure. Once they are ready, it is time to play Shark Bait. The scuba kid with the ball is to dribble through as many

2-yard gates as they can, which were set up during the water break by you and the other instructors. The instructors now become the creatures of the sea, on the hunt for scuba kids without a fish for protection. Let the players figure out how they are to survive if they are being chased by a shark. What do they need if they are to protect themselves? How are they to get a fish and perform the shark defense? Hopefully the players will answer you and say how they need to get the fish (soccer ball) from their partner and perform shark defense. Start the game and coach as you chase. Ask players to locate their teammate and communicate as to get the fish. Then be patient as they perform the skill. Once the defense is used, go chase after another scuba kid. After all players have been chased a few times, change from a shark to another sea creature you worked on and play again. Make sure players are counting the gates they travel through so those who are not being chased are active. Once we have gone through all sea creatures and the scuba kids have a good level of success, send them away for a water break.

Part 3: Great news, instructors, our fishes have located the sunken pirate ship full of gold and jewels. Now it is time to set the scuba kids free as they collect as much booty as they can. Separate the players into teams and create a square at every corner, one for every team. Place the soccer balls in the middle, equidistant from each team, and explain how the skirmish for the treasure works. Players are to line up behind the farthest cone and will come to the treasure soccer balls one at a time from each line. Players must perform a specific maneuver to take a ball, otherwise they will have to put the ball back and try again. Use skills previously used in the session to reinforce the skills for today. Once all of the treasure has gone from the middle, do a quick count up and get the balls back in the middle as we move on to the next skill. Once all the skills have been reiterated, allow the scuba kids to steal treasure from other team's scuba bases, but only after explaining the rules:

1. Nobody is allowed to try and take the treasure away from someone.
2. Nobody is allowed to defend their base.
3. A player must use a skill done during the session to take the treasure from a base.
4. Only one piece of treasure can be taken at a time.

Allow all players to play at the same time and let them play. Make sure we have an instructor at each base whenever possible, otherwise try your best to enforce the rules, especially the use of skill to take a ball. Once the players become fatigued, start the countdown to the end of the game. If you are like me, you have tried to wait until the weakest group has the most balls in their area before calling the game to an end. Do a quick count-up and send the players away for a water break.

Part 4: Now is the time to get players to use the skills in a game format. Create two teams and have them on a field with goals at each end, as you would see on game days. Have all the treasure under your possession around the halfway line off the field and be ready to play score the treasure. Our scuba kids have won treasure for themselves; however they must get it home if they are to be rich. Players will get points for scoring goals, but more importantly, by performing skills learned throughout the eight weeks.

Go crazy whenever a player gets a point with a skill, and slightly react when a player scores. This should encourage more skill opposed to scoring. When a ball goes out of bounds, get a ball to the weaker players to give them an opportunity for brilliance. After every player performs a skill, bring the players in and tell all the players how amazing they are with specific instances in the game. Send the players away, and I hope you have enjoyed a great season!

Now is time to get the coaches in for their final meeting of the season. Firstly, reward the winner of the skills competition. Hopefully you were brought to tears of joy over the weekend with teams producing miracle, skill-based performances. From here, we can challenge the coaches further by creating a competition every week, whereas now we can work on the base level score for each team. For instance, if team A scored 45 skills on the weekend and team B scored 12, the team that has the better differential of skill will win. Therefore if team A completes 47, and team B completes 17 the following week, team B will win, because they scored five more skills than they did last week. Team A only scored two more skills, so they lose. This will give lower ability teams a reason to compete because so often a team will lose every game of a season and the morale goes down. Other ideas, such as the cumulative skill score of both teams on a field will be scored against other fields (team A skill score + team B skill score = 99 on field 1. Team C skill score + team D skill score = 78 on field 2. Field 1 wins). Many systems can be used, but try and find a way to keep competition between the coaches, but directed on skill development, not goals scored. You can choose to do this on the last week of play or to let the reigns loose and let the coaches do whatever they want. You know your coaches the best, so do whatever you feel is right. Ask them what they think if you wish, but understand that if you want the coaches back, take care of their needs.

Thank the coaches for all the hard work they have done and how the program has been a success purely because of them. It is time to give credit to the people that make youth programs happen. You cannot thank and reward these people enough, so see if the organization can do something for them, or ask the parents to chip in and get them a little token of appreciation. A team picture specifically for the coach or any gesture is great to show them they are appreciated. Imagine next season without them, and you will understand their value to the program!

SESSION TOPIC	KEY COACHING POINTS
Under the Sea Adventure (Ball mastery)	1. Use the correct technique 2. Fast feet 3. Head and eyes up

Session Story: Our soccer players are swimming under the sea, avoiding sharks, an octopus, stingrays, killer whales, piranhas, and lots of other deadly creatures as they search for the treasures of the sea. Their ball mastery skills may save them from the creatures under the water, but who will score the most treasure?

SWIM LIKE FISH

We create our underwater area where no one can leave unless they hold their breath. (They can breathe once more when they return to the playing area.) The players dribble their fish (the ball) around in many directions. When the coach calls out a body part, the player has to stop the squiggly fish with a part of their body. As we learn how to swim, the coach teaches ball mastery skills which help protect us from the deadly creatures of the sea. For example, "forward push stop" is the "shark defense."

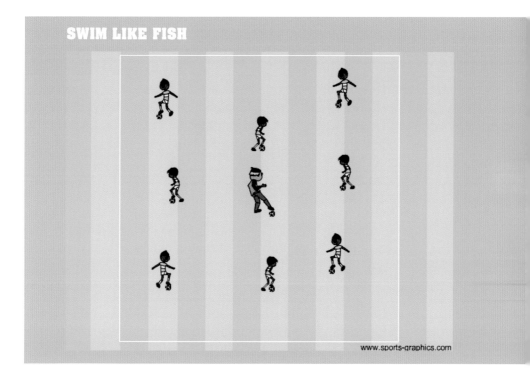

SWIM LIKE FISH

www.sports-graphics.com

Coaching points: 1. Use the correct technique

2. Fast feet.

3. Head and eyes up

SHARK BAIT

The players are split up into two teams and paired up with a player on the opposition. Each pair has a ball between them. When a player has the ball, they are protected from the sharks and the other player is shark bait, chased after by the shark (the coach). When the player has the ball he or she is trying to get away and score as many points as possible by dribbling through gates, which are around the area, while the other player is trying to get the soccer ball to protect themselves from the shark. After 1v1, move to team versus team.

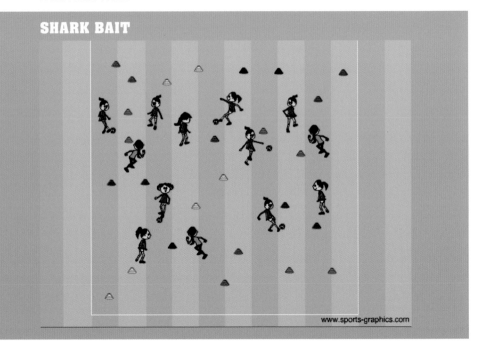

SHARK BAIT

www.sports-graphics.com

Coaching points: 1. Keep your body between the defender and the ball

2. Keep your head up to be aware of where the defender is

3. Move into the space away from the defender and through the gates

TREASURE HUNT

All the soccer balls are pieces of valuable treasure on a sunken ship. Players are swimming down to the ship and taking the treasure back to their base. When all the treasure is taken from the sunken ship, the players can go and steal the treasure from each other's bases. The whole time the players must be aware of the deadly creatures swimming around the ocean and use their moves taught earlier in the adventure to get away from them.

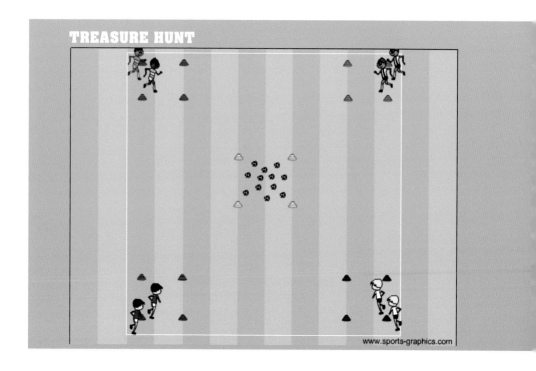

Coaching points: 1. Use the correct technique

2. Fast feet.

3. Head and eyes up

SCORE THE TREASURE

Now we have all the treasure we need to get it home. Each team is defending the opposition's home, and they play a normal game of soccer. The team who scores the most treasure at the end is the winner. Multiple pieces of treasure may be in the area at one time, and boundaries are not necessary for the younger age players. Add skill development to get the skills used in the session out in the game

SCORE THE TREASURE

www.sports-graphics.com

Coaching points: 1. Have Fun!

2. Have Fun!

3. Have Fun!

CHAPTER EIGHT

CREATING COACHABLE PLAYERS: CONVERTING THE SESSION INTO THE GAME

CREATING COACHABLE PLAYERS: CONVERTING THE SESSION INTO THE GAME

Game day is why we teach all the skills, but what do we do as coaches to bridge the gap between a practice session and the game? How can we believe that whatever we teach in a practice environment can be instantly replicated in the game without our assistance?

My years of working summer camps prove this point magnificently. I teach so much to the children, come back a year later, and the majority of their skills have disappeared. They have not used what was taught to them. Before long, the body and brain forget. It is easier to bring them back to speed, but then the same thing happens again the following year. We are left asking, "How long are we away from them before they forget?"

How often should we revisit the same skill before they have the skill forever? Is it a year, a month, a week, a day? The answer is: It is different for every child. However, if a player is successful using a skill in a game environment, then the chance of the child remembering the skill is significantly increased. We need to encourage the use of any skill we teach, regardless of its use in an actual game. If a player performs toe taps in a game, you may say this is pointless. But now the child has gained confidence on the ball in a game-like environment. The player quite possibly looked around the field while performing the technique and made a wise decision. To me, this is 10 times better than a successful pass. From here, the player will have the confidence to try different skills and will do more of what the coach asks. This makes him or her a more coachable player at the same time.

More food for thought: Are there just the three stages of player development or should there be more?

As coaches on the "certification path to success," you will hear the words unopposed (no pressure), semi-opposed (limited pressure), and opposed (full pressure) or similar. This means, when teaching the skill to a person with no prior knowledge, we first teach with no pressure or opposition, then we add gradual pressure until they are fully opposed in a game-like setting. From there we throw the players into a game and ask them to replicate what they did in training on the field. To me, this is a little unrealistic. The players are looking to put the ball in the back of the net, not listen to a coach.

At the older ages especially, we teach them to win, win, and win. It is difficult for them to see our full vision of how we would like them to play. They have memories of what they have done in the past and what works for them. Therefore, that is exactly what they do. The more tactics are involved, the more we need all the players to be on the same page. One player simply doing what they want will ruin the balance of the whole team. So how do we get the players to believe in us and in what we say? If we have success in training, this may bubble over to the field, but what have we done in the early ages to make this happen? I believe there are two stages missing: semi-opposed in the game and opposed in the game.

For these two stages, we need to look at the game not as a win/lose opportunity, but as the final session of the week. We have done the first three stages of player development. Now it's time for the fourth and fifth stages. During these sessions, we would like them to find an area of space on the game field and perform the skill we have taught that week. Once they have done this on the field, we ask them to use the skill for a purpose. This generally means they will go against the opposition to either beat the player or to create space.

From here, we can teach the tactics of when and where to use the skill, the correct foot to use in each situation, and why. We can address the purpose of performing the skill as well as the success the player would have had if the skill isn't quite executed properly. We can also point out the success the player gained when it did work. We have now taken the skill from zero knowledge to achieving our goal of using the skill proficiently in a game environment versus another team. Once the player gains enough success with the skill, the maneuver becomes ingrained into the players muscle memory and becomes a natural act. The players will get themselves into an area of trouble on the field and instantly use a skill without thinking to get themselves out of danger. This is where we want to take our players, and only once we achieve this success will our coaching be fully effective. Our coaching finishes in the game, not in the practices.

CHAPTER
NINE

CONCLUSION OF DEVELOPMENT

CONCLUSION OF DEVELOPMENT

In conclusion, planning a training session for young players is not as easy as one may think but can become simple and successful with a little pre-planning. There are a few factors which need to be considered. First, pick a topic you wish to cover (90-degree turns, for example). Then, select the games which you know you will be successful at teaching the topic. Next, select an adventure, like Robot Wars for example, and create a story. Finally, have fun with the players! The more fun YOU have, the more fun the session is for the children. Remember, we do not stop there.

Regardless of the session, I hope you have fun with your players and take pride in being an educator. Not everyone accepts the position of youth coach with ease of conviction. Most youth organizations are contacting parents, begging them for their help, but you are a gift to these children for accepting the role. Once you understand the difference you are making to these young people's lives, you cannot help but feel a massive sense of pride. Hopefully with this book you can also understand how you are gifting these players with a love for the sport of soccer through tangible success. Once you see your first player perform a skill you taught them in a game, you will be jumping for joy as the overwhelming sense of pride rushes through your body. The part we do not see is the same sense of pride and accomplishment that is rushing through the player also. That pride may keep the player in a game they may love forever, and what can be better than that?

I WISH YOU ALL THE LUCK AND
FUN IN THE WORLD WITH YOUR PLAYERS!

Credits

Copyediting: Elizabeth Evans

Layout and typesetting: Kristina Ehrhardt

Coverdesign: Sabine Groten

Graphics: easy Sports-Graphics, www.easy-sports-software.com

Photos: Kim Castell